Assignment & Thesis

Writing

3 RD EDITION

JONATHAN ANDERSON | MILLICENT POOLE

John Wiley & Sons Australia Ltd

BRISBANE • NEW YORE • TORONTO

Third edition published 1998 by
John Wiley & Sons Australia, Ltd
33 Park Road, Milton, Qld 4064

Offices also in Sydney and Melbourne

First edition 1970
Second edition 1994

Typeset in 10/11.5 pt Times

© John Wiley & Sons Australia, Ltd 1970, 1994, 1998

National Library of Australia
Cataloguing-in-Publication data

Anderson, Jonathan, 1939–   .
    Assignment and thesis writing.

    3rd ed.
    Bibliography.
    Includes index.
    ISBN 0 471 33927 X.

    1. Dissertations, Academic. 2. Report writing. I. Poole,
    Millicent E. (Millicent Eleanor). II. Title.

808.06

Cover design by Kate Barry

Cover photo: The Image Bank/Pierre-Yves Goavec

Printed in Singapore

10 9 8 7 6 5 4 3

FOREWORD

Foreword to the Second Edition

When I wrote my honours thesis, at the University of New England in 1958, there was no guide to would-be thesis writers other than the example of the theses of previous honours students, and in our department of history there was only one of those. A year later, preparing a master's thesis in history, I used as my model of presentation the thesis of the most successful of my colleagues in our own honours year. A decade or so later, at Macquarie University, I wrote a few pages of advice on essay and assignment writing for students in politics, mostly because I had not then come across the first edition of this most useful book.

The purpose of all scholastic apparatus is to conceal itself. It is there to speed the message of your assignment or thesis. The reader should not have to puzzle about matters of presentation: references, footnotes, tables and figures, paragraphs and chapters — all are there to aid speedy understanding. A common style in these matters is a great help not only to the individual student, but to the intellectual community itself. That is the moral of *Assignment and Thesis Writing*.

That the book is still in print a quarter of a century after its genesis certainly says a lot for its value. Who would have thought in 1970 that a later edition would include a chapter on 'Computer Tools for Writers'? Who would then have known what 'Scanners' or 'Spreadsheets' were, or 'CD-ROM'? And who would be without them today! I welcome the new edition, and commend it to a new generation of grateful users.

Don Aitkin, Vice-Chancellor, University of Canberra
January 1994

Foreword to the Third Edition

Technology never remains still, and the Internet and the World Wide Web now provide valuable, new tools for students and researchers. Developed first by the military, then adopted by academic researchers, and now in wide use by the general public, the Internet and the Web produced the need for a further edition to this valuable book. Students and researchers now need to know not only about URLs but also how to reference new sources of information available via the Internet. The inclusion in this edition of guidelines for citing and referencing electronic media and online sources, as well as the new chapter on the computer as information tool, will be invaluable to yet further generations of grateful users.

Don Aitkin, Vice-Chancellor, University of Canberra
July 1997

ACKNOWLEDGMENTS

Many people have contributed to the revision of this book. We are indebted to all those who offered expert advice and critical comment. Special thanks are due to Richard Grice from the University of Queensland with whom many discussions about editorial style and consistency were held. John Keeves from Flinders University and Greg Martin from Text+Design provided valuable comments during the revision.

We wish to express our gratitude to the research assistants who worked on the project. In particular, we thank Maria Mulcahy for helpful work on many chapters, Vicki Englund for her research on qualitative research procedures and Sam Nielsen for his assistance in proof reading.

For the cartoons we thank Ross Anderson while for other graphical material thanks are due to Michael Fardon and Joy Noble. Our many students, undergraduate and graduate, who have used this text since it first appeared in 1970, have also contributed in valuable ways.

Every effort has been made to trace the ownership of copyright material. Holders of information that will enable the publisher to rectify any error or omission in subsequent editions will be welcome to contact the Permissions Department of the publisher. In these instances, the publisher will be happy to pay the usual permissions fee to the copyright holder.

TABLE OF
CONTENTS

Part II Writing the Assignment or Thesis

Appendixes

LIST OF TABLES

LIST OF FIGURES

Part I

ASSIGNMENTS AND THESES AT THE TERTIARY LEVEL

Chapter 1

WRITING AT THE
TERTIARY LEVEL

Written work is an integral part of a university education. Assignments and research papers perform an invaluable function in prompting students to think independently about issues and subjects. Students also learn how to access, select and evaluate information from different sources and to formulate ideas.

At the tertiary level there has been growing dissatisfaction with reliance upon examinations as the sole (or major) means of evaluating student performance. At most universities considerable weight is given to evidence of student progress throughout a course measured by regular tests and assignments rather than to a single, do-or-die examination. The benefits of continuous assessment to students and lecturers hardly need amplification here. It is sufficient to note the trend and to recognise that, if students are required to submit essays, assignments, tutorial papers, reports, dissertations or theses as evidence of independent study, it is important that such material be well written. Many students confronted with tasks that demand good writing skills are under prepared and often unaware of the range of electronic tools to aid writers. They need guidance in how to go about the complex job of writing assignments and theses. This book presents just such a guide.

Assignments and Term Papers

Typically, written assignments and term papers are geared to course work covered by a series of lectures or tutorials (although sometimes essays are set in an endeavour to cover important aspects of a subject not covered by lectures or tutorials). Students are assigned a particular topic to write about or given a list of topics from which to choose. They receive instructions as to the length of the essay and the due date for submission. Some guidance may be given to students in the form of a suggested reading list. In courses that are well planned, lecturers usually inform students of their written work commitments for the full course at the beginning of the semester so that students can plan their study program effectively.

The topics set for written assignments may give a useful guide to important content areas of a course of study. Assignments encourage students to read critically in a particular content area, to search for and select from available material, to organise their thoughts on a topic, and to submit to the discipline of communicating their thoughts through the presentation of evidence that they have sifted and evaluated to arrive at certain conclusions. Apart from learning the subject matter of a course, this process of independent study has considerable educational value.

Essay writing is a means of gaining valuable experience in examination technique, since examiners in many institutions continue to rely heavily on the essay question as a form of examination. However, unlike the typical examination that tends to produce stressful situations, most written assignments or term papers give students plenty of time to plan and organise their work. Students do not have to depend on hurried recall of material covered in lectures or textbooks, but are given the opportunity to plan carefully, to read widely, to compose their thoughts, and to commit them to paper in an acceptable way. A much higher quality of work therefore is expected.

An essay does not normally require original research. It is an exercise that is usually seen only by the student and the marker and is not shelved in the library for public scrutiny. The marker is expected to write comments on the paper for the guidance of the student so that the student can use these comments for remedial purposes. Therefore, the essay is a relatively personal document that is used as much for learning and teaching as for examining.

Theses and Dissertations

Students enrolled for an honours degree, a postgraduate diploma or a higher degree are almost invariably required to submit a thesis or dissertation. There is no generally held agreement about the terms *thesis* and *dissertation*. Often the two terms are used interchangeably. In this book they are taken to be synonymous.

A thesis is much more than a large term paper. It normally represents the culmination of a substantial piece of original work over a period of at least a year. Some research replicates previous research with the object of testing the reported findings of that research or testing the relevance of findings of research completed in a different cultural milieu. Other research builds on existing studies to follow up new leads or to refine or qualify the findings of earlier studies. In either case, the thesis is expected to make an original contribution to knowledge.

Students embarking on a thesis are usually much more responsible for selecting and delimiting an area of study than are students writing assignments or essays. However, it is not uncommon for students commencing a thesis to be given a topic or to be guided into areas that are of special interest to faculty members with whom they will work. Indeed, students may seek enrolment in a particular university because of the special interests of the faculty there.

Outside examiners are usually engaged to assess theses and, once a thesis is accepted, a bound copy is placed in the library of the institution conferring the degree. Thesis abstracts are published and scholars throughout the world may borrow the thesis on interlibrary loan. The thesis virtually becomes public property. The reputations of the student, the faculty, and the institution itself, are at stake. Standards set for theses must, therefore, be much higher than those set for essays.

Conventions of Writing – A Question of Style

Some key differences between written assignments and theses are outlined above. An assignment is more limited in scope and shorter than a thesis, and it is less likely to involve original research. However, these differences do not relate as much to form as to nature and scope. Indeed, correct form is as important in the presentation of a written assignment as it is in a thesis. Similarly, both assignments and theses require the use of scholarly style, and so most of the recommendations in this section apply to all writing at university.

Authorities have reached no absolute agreement regarding details of form in thesis writing. In any particular situation, several different forms may be acceptable. Some teaching departments require theses to follow special forms quite different from those required elsewhere. For example, a department of sociology may require students to use a particular referencing technique that would not be acceptable to the department of history at the same university, or to the department of sociology at another institution. The thesis writer should find out the requirements of a particular department. The student also is counselled to read widely on the special problems of form and style in thesis writing, paying particular reference to the subject area of the thesis. Account should be taken of special departmental requirements to achieve a standardised form of referencing, footnoting, presenting tables, and so on. A list of resources for writers is included in this chapter. Regardless of the particular system adopted, once the format to be used is determined, the student must be consistent throughout the thesis. Thus, while the content of the thesis is important, the presentation of the argument in a standard form is a discipline that is vital to its acceptability. Good research may be marred by poor reporting; proper presentation is an integral part of the whole project.

Research can become a contribution to a field of knowledge only when it is adequately communicated. For this purpose, precise writing is essential. A careful choice of words will serve to convey exact meaning. The best word to express an idea is not necessarily the longest word. A thesaurus (e.g. the *Macquarie Thesaurus*) is an invaluable reference. Terms should be clearly defined at the outset and their use must be consistent with such definitions.

Colloquial, conversational and subjective, highly personalised modes of expression are inappropriate in a thesis. Avoid abbreviations such as *&* and *don't* (although abbreviations are acceptable in tables). Scientific writing is not of a personal or conversational nature and for this reason the third person is commonly used. As a general rule, personal pronouns such as *I, we, you, me, my, our* and *us* should not appear except in quotations. A thesis should not consist of the reporting of personal experience or opinion, but should be a critical analysis of a problem and the presentation of evidence relating to that problem, and this is better arrived at by using a tone of scientific impersonality.

At the same time the thesis writer should strive for a high level of readability. Avoid sentences that are too involved or complex. Scholarly writing is not crammed with jargon. Avoid antiquated language:

Use *while* instead of *whilst*;
   although rather than *albeit*.

Verbose, ambiguous, pedantic or pompous writing is not scholarly. Nor are sweeping statements and exaggerated claims scholarly. Statements must be suitably qualified or supported. Sound reasoning and intellectual honesty are hallmarks of scholarly style. Quotations must be accurately cited and suitably acknowledged. The contributions of other writers must be duly recognised. The extent and nature of the thesis writer's contribution then are more readily apparent.

Since a thesis recounts what has already been done, it is written in the past tense. While this does not altogether preclude the use of the present and future tenses, the thesis writer should have a good reason for using these tenses. Note that the present tense is always used – never the future tense – to indicate where topics or materials are located in a thesis:

The literature is reviewed in Chapter 2.
Copies of test instruments are reproduced in
Appendix B.

Accurate spelling is essential for scholarly writing. This applies both to common words and proper names. Consult an authoritative dictionary (e.g. the *Macquarie*) for correct spelling, and in the case of proper names, the best available authority. Pay particular attention to grammar and punctuation. Several excellent references are listed in this chapter. Where there is more than one spelling of a word, the writer should try to be consistent:

Use either "s" or "z" spellings throughout (*organise* or *organize*).

Students should be aware of differences between Australian and American spelling. The 's' form is the preferred Australian form in the *Macquarie Dictionary*. Other examples of preferred spellings occur in words like:

centre (not center)
colour (not color)
behaviour (not behavior)

However, if quoting from an American source, use the exact spelling of the original. Some university departments may express a preference for a particular spelling style. Where no policy is laid down, the best rule to follow is *be consistent*.

Scholarly writing avoids the use of sexist language, stereotyping and ethnic bias. Thus writers need consciously to use language that is gender neutral and avoid, for instance, the use of *man* as a generic noun:

Use *people* or *human species* in place of *man*.

Similarly, it is preferable to avoid the pronouns *he* or *she* to refer to, say, *the teacher* or *the therapist*:

Use instead the plural *teachers* and *therapists* followed by *they*.

Patterns of language change over time when reference is made to ethnic groups. Writers need to find out what is currently acceptable terminology:

The term *Eskimo* is rejected by those to whom it commonly refers. The preferred reference is now *Inuit*.

Resources for Writers

When writing assignments or theses, students need to find out if there are specific departmental requirements and, of course, follow any instructions from lecturers or tutors. For those who wish to read further, there are several useful reference books that complement this guide.

A short list of essential resources for writers might include books of English expression such as Fowler's *Dictionary of Modern English Usage* and Murray-Smith's *Right Words: A Guide to English Usage in Australia*. To these should be added an authoritative dictionary such as the *Macquarie Dictionary* and a thesaurus, perhaps the *Macquarie Thesaurus*. A general style manual for checking particular aspects of writing and editorial style would also find a place on any short list. One produced specifically for use in Australia is the *Style Manual for Authors, Editors and Printers*. Finally, a short list might include a style manual for particular fields such as those available for biology, geography, psychology, and other disciplines.

Appendix A contains a more complete list of useful resources for writers, together with publishing details.

How to Read this Guide

This guide is in three parts. The first part, of which this chapter is the introduction, deals with the nature of assignments and theses at the tertiary level. The planning of written assignments and theses is considered separately in the next two chapters which are in turn followed by a case study of a student's research paper. Chapters 5 and 6 detail the range of electronic tools that can assist in all phases of research from locating information through to writing, documenting, editing, and printing. It is useful to read through Part I at the earliest opportunity to learn what are the characteristics of scholarly writing. As illustrated in Chapters 4, 5 and 6, preparation for writing needs to begin early.

Part II of the book deals with features of editorial style (Chapter 7), with the general format of written essays and reports or longer theses (Chapter 8), and with guidelines for commonly accepted conventions such as page and chapter format (Chapter 9). Further chapters document the use of quotations (Chapter 10), footnoting (Chapter 11), layout of tables and figures (Chapter 12), referencing (Chapter 13) and appendixes (Chapter 14). It is useful to skim read these chapters and then return to them during the writing and revision stages. Adopting scholarly conventions of writing at the outset helps to provide a framework for writing. The logic and argument of a set or selected topic can then be the primary focus of attention.

Ways to edit and evaluate a paper are covered in Part III. While this might seem to be a section to leave until the final stages of writing, the checklists contained in Chapter 15 are helpful to refer to when beginning to write. The best advice, then, is to read the book right through before returning to focus on particular chapters.

PLANNING THE ASSIGNMENT

This chapter describes key tasks in planning written assignments that, at the undergraduate level, usually require students to write on a set topic or to choose from a list of suggested topics. Occasionally, at the second and third year level, students may be required to choose a topic in consultation with their lecturer or tutor. Whatever the case may be, the first task is to define and limit the problem.

Further tasks in planning are to acknowledge any limitations and to determine a time schedule. A major allocation of time will be for consulting source material and collecting information, and suggestions are given for preparing a working bibliography, whether on cards or computer, and taking notes. Care needs to be taken when quoting and paraphrasing to acknowledge the work of other researchers appropriately.

Defining the Problem

Defining the problem involves determining what the question, assignment or essay requires. A dictionary should be consulted to define key terms in the topic. Some commonly encountered words and their different shades of meaning are listed below:

1. *Analyse*: consider the various components of the whole and try to describe the inter-relationships between them.
2. *Compare*: examine the characteristics of the objects in question to demonstrate their similarities and their differences.
3. *Contrast*: examine the characteristics of the objects in question to demonstrate differences.
4. *Define*: give a definition or state terms of reference.

5. *Describe*: give an account of.
6. *Discuss*: present the different aspects of a question or problem.
7. *Enumerate*: give a listing.
8. *Evaluate*: examine the various sides of a question and try to reach a judgment.
9. *Examine critically*: act as a judge or critic, appraise.
10. *Illustrate*: give an example, explain, draw a figure.
11. *Prove*: demonstrate or show by logical argument.
12. *Summarise*: state the main points briefly.

For almost every subject there are special dictionaries of technical terms. Subject specific dictionaries are excellent research tools, particularly for students planning specialised study in an area. Consult such dictionaries to define all terms used in, or necessary for, the assignment or essay question. This procedure assists students in clarifying their thoughts and provides an ideal starting point for the assignment. Clear definition of terms is one of the hallmarks of scholarly writing.

Limiting the Problem

A common mistake with undergraduate assignments (and with many graduate theses and dissertations) is to be too ambitious and to attempt topics that are far too broad. The mistake of casting the net wide is an understandable one because a common reaction when starting an assignment is to wonder how one could possibly write the required number of words. After some initial reading, however, most students find the reverse problem – there is too much to write. Hence, time spent at the outset in limiting a problem, or defining its limits (sometimes called a *statement of delimitations*), is usually rewarded.

A problem is not delimited by omitting important information, leaving out essential details, or presenting only part of the evidence. Rather, a problem is delimited by reducing the scope of the investigation. Consider, for example, the following topics:

1. Diseases Affecting Wheat
2. The Control of Rust in Wheat
3. Recent Developments in the Control of Rust in Wheat in the Darling Downs Region.

The first topic is sufficient scope for a book. Even the second topic is far too broad to deal with adequately in a term paper. The third topic is beginning to reach manageable proportions. Failure to limit the problem at the outset can lead to the collection of a mass of data, much of which ultimately needs to be discarded, or worse, can lead to a somewhat superficial treatment. A clear statement fixing or marking the limits of a study or investigation is another hallmark of scholarly writing.

Specifying the Limitations

Not to be confused with defining limits (delimitations of a study) is a statement of a study's *limitations*. In any investigation there are conditions imposed from without, restrictions or shortcomings that ideally would not be present. Students need to acknowledge any limitations inherent in conducting a study on a particular topic.

A study in a particular field may be limited, for example, by access (travel may only be possible at certain times), or because information is not available (certain records may not be publicly accessible). For case studies, limitations may exist because of the policies of an organisation (information may be made available to professionals in the field but not to students in training). Other limitations may include a time frame within which the study will focus, or may be imposed by reason of the study needing to be completed within a given period. In experimental work, limitations may be imposed by restricted access to equipment, whereas in field studies, environmental conditions may govern when and where data are collected.

Nearly all studies have some of the kinds of limitations described above. It is not only important, but a strength to acknowledge such restraints frankly.

A Time Schedule

Assignments are marked on the final product presented. It seems sensible, then, that considerable care and attention be devoted to presentation. Unfortunately, too many assignments look as though they were written in haste the night before. Regrettably, many of them are. This failure to schedule time appropriately usually results in an inferior piece of writing.

Table 2.1 presents a suggested allocation of time for different stages of writing that may be used as a guide.

Table 2.1 Time allocation for different stages of writing

Stages of writing	Time allocation
Defining and limiting problem, specifying limitations, consulting source material, and collecting information	60%
First draft	20%
Revising, footnoting, referencing, writing the final draft, proofreading	20%

Table 2.1 presents a very general time allocation and not all the activities will be applicable to all assignments. It does, however, emphasise the importance of writing, revising and polishing the finer points in the total assignment, as well as the need for careful planning.

Consulting Source Material

A suggested list of references is often included with set assignments. This is a valuable starting point for research and these references should be consulted first. When many students are enrolled in a course, a particular reference is frequently not readily available. Thus it is necessary to begin reading early and to take notes (see *Taking Notes*, pages 14–16).

Reference books themselves contain further references and these, if held by the institution's library, often provide promising leads. Students soon learn who are the accepted authorities within a field, and this helps in the evaluation of material read.

Another useful method for locating source material for a particular topic is to check the library shelves or catalogue for books having the same classification number as other books to which reference has been made. Suppose, for example, that an assignment has been set on animal inbreeding. One of the suggested references has a Dewey classification of 575.133. Consult other books that have the same Dewey classification. When these have been exhausted, look at books further up the hierarchy at 575.13 that deal with factors affecting heredity. Even books further up the hierarchy at 575.1 on genetics, and further up still at 575 on organic evolution, may have useful chapters or sections on the set topic. References have a tendency to increase rapidly, and more than ever there is a need for careful evaluation.

In addition, there are a number of other sources that might provide relevant information. These include encyclopedias, handbooks, yearbooks, indexes, abstracts, atlases and newspapers. Another most valuable source of reading, particularly for the student in the social and other sciences, is journal articles. Academic and professional journals contain more up-to-date information than that contained in books, and this makes them essential reading in a number of subject areas.

A new source of information that can be immensely useful when you are looking for the most current and up-to-date information is the Internet and the World Wide Web. So important has the Web, as it is familiarly called, become that a separate chapter (see Chapter 6) is devoted to this information source.

Preparing a Working Bibliography

A bibliography for a written assignment is an alphabetic list of all source material to which reference has been made. There are different ways of referencing books, journal articles, and other documents, and this topic is dealt with in detail in Chapter 13. However, the essential information required for all references is:

1. author's surname and initials and date of publication
2. the name of the article and/or journal or book
3. the imprint (publisher and place of publication).

Since a working bibliography is being prepared, it is useful to add three further items of information:

4. the call number of the book or journal
5. the library where the book or journal may be located
6. a phrase or sentence indicating its contents.

In the case of electronic or online sources of information special considerations apply, but two further items need to be recorded:

7. the URL of the Web page
8. the date you accessed the information.

Using Cards

Many students find it useful to write each reference of the working bibliography on 7 × 12.5 cm cards because these are easy to sort alphabetically and to store. A resulting set of cards is called a working bibliography because new cards can be added, constant reference is made to existing cards, and additions and corrections to cards may be noted. A typical reference card is shown in Figure 2.1.

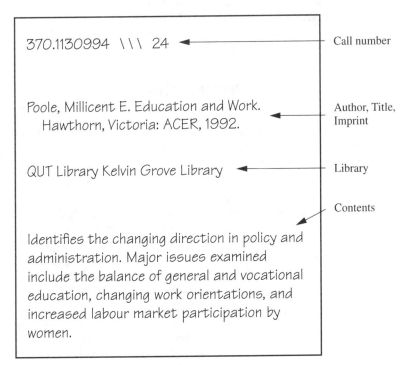

Figure 2.1 Typical reference card with details of library call number and publishing information

The use of a card bibliography saves time. If a book or journal needs to be consulted again, no time is lost in searching for the call number. New references can be added to the sequence easily. Cards can be compiled in the library and are easily carried from place to place. On completion, a bibliography can be compiled directly from the information recorded on the cards.

On Computer

Students may find a personal computer an easy and efficient way of recording references during their research for an assignment. The advantage of computers is that information can be easily accessed and, with information filed on floppy disk, a bibliographic system is quite portable. Using a computer to record bibliographic details, students can enter information and then rearrange it later. Some computer programs can sort references alphabetically. Even without such programs, it is an easy task to rearrange references on screen and insert information where necessary.

Although using a computer to prepare a working bibliography has certain advantages, a card system for recording and arranging information is still an easy and convenient method of researching.

The use of computers and other electronic tools for preparing assignments and theses is presented in greater detail in Chapter 5 while Chapter 6 deals with the computer as an information tool.

Taking Notes

Again it is useful to make notes on cards. Something a little larger than the bibliographic card is recommended – either 10×15 cm or 12.5×20 cm cards are best. Here are some suggestions for taking notes:

1. *Use a separate card for each idea, fact or concept.* This enables cards to be sorted into categories and attached to the draft outline. In subsequent redrafts, much writing time is saved.
2. *Put a heading at the top of each card.* Such headings usually consist of key words or phrases to help identify the note without having to read it through.
3. *Record sufficient information to identify each note.* Since a working bibliography has previously been prepared, the name of the author and date are sufficient to identify the publication. To locate the note within a publication, the page number also is required.
4. *Indicate where information has been paraphrased or quoted.* Checking the accuracy of quotes when taking notes saves considerable time at a later stage. Words omitted from a sentence are indicated by ellipsis marks:

   "Books ... propose to instruct or to amuse."
   Thomas de Quincey

The modern convention is to use ellipsis without a period even if words are omitted at the end of a sentence:

"People seldom read a book which is given ..."
Dr Samuel Johnson

If any words are added to a quote to make it intelligible out of its original context, the additional words are enclosed in square brackets:

"[Henry Fielding] whose works it has long been the fashion to abuse in public and to read in secret."
George Borrow

Chapter 10 provides a more complete discussion of the conventions for quoting from the work of other writers.

The sample card notes in Figures 2.2 and 2.3 illustrate some of the points made above. If there is too much information for one card, it may be continued on a second and the cards labelled a, b, ... and so on.

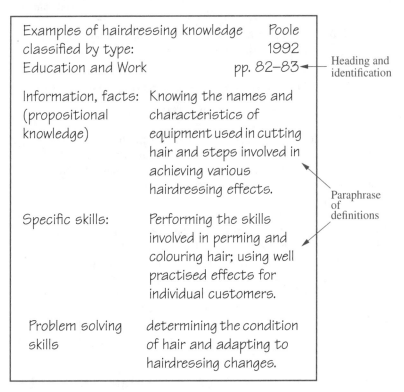

Examples of hairdressing knowledge   Poole
classified by type: 1992
Education and Work   pp. 82–83 ←— Heading and identification

Information, facts: Knowing the names and
(propositional   characteristics of
knowledge)   equipment used in cutting
                      hair and steps involved in
                      achieving various
                      hairdressing effects.
                                              — Paraphrase of definitions
Specific skills: Performing the skills
                      involved in perming and
                      colouring hair; using well
                      practised effects for
                      individual customers.

Problem solving   determining the condition
skills   of hair and adapting to
                      hairdressing changes.

Figure 2.2 Bibliographic card with heading to identify note and showing source of information

Education and Work	Poole 1992 — Heading and identification
	p. 15
	Ellipsis for words omitted at beginning of sentence
"... it is in the national interest to facilitate the entry of women to areas of the workplace which have critical [although self-inflicted] skills shortages, e.g. technicians and technologists".	Three words inserted in quote indicated by [ ]
	Quoted verbatim

Figure 2.3 Bibliographic card for a quote indicating source and any omitted or added words

Quoting and Paraphrasing versus Plagiarism

When taking notes, paraphrases or summaries can be combined with verbatim quotes but always use quotation marks for direct quotes. It is too easy later to forget that certain phrases belong to other writers and so be guilty of plagiarism. An author's ideas, even if stated in other words, need to be acknowledged.

Plagiarism is generally defined as the deliberate incorporation in an essay or paper of material drawn from the work of another person without acknowledgment. The penalty for plagiarising is high: in some departments it results in a failure for the essay and sometimes an automatic failure in a course. Yet a narrow line often separates plagiarism from good scholarship. In scholarly writing, it is nearly always essential to refer to the work of others. Since an essay, assignment or project is individual work, it is important to document any indebtedness in the appropriate way.

A quotation from the paragraph above, for example, might be acknowledged in the following way:

Anderson and Poole (1998, p. 16) state that "... a narrow line often separates plagiarism from good scholarship."

A paraphrase of the same idea, on the other hand, could be acknowledged as follows:

A subtle distinction often exists between plagiarism and good scholarship (Anderson and Poole 1998, p. 16).

The correct use of quotations and accurate referencing in acknowledging the work of others, detailed further in Chapters 10 and 13, are evidence of scholarly writing.

The Outline

An outline may take many forms and certain teaching departments may specify particular formats. Students should be familiar with departmental requirements. The following is a suggested outline that may be used as a guide.

Introduction

Give a clear statement of the problem. Define terms and indicate the limits of the study and any limitations. Set the problem within a meaningful background. This may take several forms: the setting of the study may be described, previous research reviewed, and the expected contribution of the study indicated. The introduction should provide the reader with all necessary information for what is to follow. Try to keep this section crisp and informative.

Body

This section should be a logical development of an argument or a particular point of view. It should be an attempt at a progressive solution to the problem stated in the introduction. The headings used in card notes may prove suitable as points to be developed into one or more paragraphs. Endeavour to keep this section moving – do not get lost in irrelevant detail and padding.

Conclusion

This section presents the findings of the study, and a solution or an approach to the solution of the problem initially stated. The study may of course suggest further problems for investigation. Studies usually do. Above all, the conclusion should not be a regurgitation of material already covered.

The First Draft

Armed with the assignment outline and reading notes, the next step is to write the first or rough draft. Much of the actual mechanics of writing and presentation is detailed in Part II of this book.

If time is allocated to the various research tasks as suggested in this chapter, the first draft will need to be completed well before the due date for submission of the assignment or research paper. Writers often find that, when they look at an assignment after an intervening period, it helps to highlight more clearly any deficiencies, omissions and disjointed or awkward expressions.

With the widespread use of word processors (discussed in further detail in Chapter 5), many assignments are now written on computer. While computers certainly make it easy to change the order or relocate passages of text, there is no substitute for careful planning of an argument. The first draft will generally progress more smoothly if students have a script to follow.

Chapter 3

PLANNING THE THESIS

In this chapter the process of planning a thesis is discussed. Since a thesis is a sustained argument, often detailed and quite complex, considerable preparation and planning are necessary before the initial research can begin.

During the planning stages, problems will inevitably emerge and at various key stages judgments need to be made about the feasibility of conducting a particular study. A literature review should be undertaken initially to determine the availability of sources for research on a particular topic.

Primary, secondary and tertiary sources need to be considered when planning a thesis in selected areas. In all cases, an initial proposal needs to be prepared outlining the chosen topic, research questions to be addressed, statement of thesis, detail of proposed methods and procedures, and any assumptions, limitations or delimitations.

Selecting a Topic

The selection of a suitable topic for a thesis or dissertation is in many ways the most difficult task. A thorough knowledge of a particular subject area is needed. Hence, at the honours undergraduate level, students are required to have completed a major in the subject before embarking on the thesis. At the master's and doctoral levels, it is necessary not only to have completed this earlier course work but also to have completed an honours thesis successfully and sometimes a preliminary or qualifying examination as well.

The more knowledge a student has of a particular field, the more able he or she is at detecting gaps in it, and recognising problem areas that require investigation. It is the ability to detect problems that the postgraduate student must develop, for every thesis or dissertation should set out to provide information about a particular problem. Indeed, the first question examiners usually consider when marking a thesis is: *Does it make a contribution to knowledge in this field?* Phrased another way, this question becomes: *Was there a problem to be investigated and did the thesis attempt to solve this problem?*

A Source of Problems for Investigation

One of the best sources of problems for investigation is at the forefront where research is being carried out. The closest one can get to this research is through direct contact with the personnel at a research institution. The research fellow, lecturer or professor who is active in research is usually a fund of research problems.

A close substitute for direct contact with researchers is contact with their writing, and most recent writing is contained in the journal literature. Here then is an important source of ideas signalling *gaps*, likely *future directions*, or *inconsistencies* in patterns of research findings in a particular area. A study of the recent literature in the chosen field usually will indicate problems that are currently being investigated and will suggest likely further problems for investigation.

Students should be familiar, too, with recent doctoral studies in their field of interest. Publications such as *Dissertation Abstracts*, which appears monthly (also available online — see Chapter 6), present concise summaries of doctoral dissertations submitted at most leading universities. Often these summaries conclude with suggestions for future research.

Criteria for Selecting a Topic

Once the field of interest is chosen and potential problem areas for investigation identified, a number of questions should be addressed.

Is there Adequate Supervision?

This may seem a strange question to ask about the lecturing staff at a tertiary institution, but it is an important one. With increasing specialisation, there may not be a member of faculty with the expertise or interest in a particular topic. More and more, however, there is a tendency for postgraduate students to go to institutions where particular interests have developed.

Does the Topic Really Interest You?

Most research projects take at least a year and successful completion often depends on whether the topic continues to hold interest. Lose this and the task becomes the worst kind of chore.

Can the Topic be Completed in the Required Time?

Some topics by their very nature require time to elapse before data can be collected. Longitudinal growth studies and long-term attitude studies fall into this category. However desirable these types of studies may be, they are rarely practical as thesis topics.

Is the Necessary Equipment Available?

Specialised and expensive equipment is required for many studies. Unless there is reasonable assurance that necessary equipment will be available when required, another topic may be advisable.

Are Subjects Available?

Much research, especially in the social sciences, requires the ready cooperation of subjects to submit to questionnaires or experimental treatments and testing. Many a thesis has been delayed or had its focus changed because the question of availability of subjects was not carefully considered at the outset.

Are Travel Funds Available to Locate Data Sources?

Often travel is needed for field trips to collect data, to use particular equipment or to interview subjects. Such investigations may require extensive travel; therefore costing needs to be considered.

Are Library Facilities Sufficient?

Library facilities are essential for literary or analytical research studies. A particular topic may prove unsuitable simply because there is not ready access to the requisite source materials. For example, it is common for some source material not to be made available during the lifetime of an individual or for some years after an event. Other material may not be held at a particular library and because of its value may not be available on inter-library loan.

Is the Study Achievable?

Another question to consider is whether the research techniques for testing a particular problem have been developed or are sufficiently refined. This question implies that the student should determine the techniques to be used before embarking upon a study.

Is the Problem a Significant One?

Whether a problem is significant is never an easy question for its answer requires considering the practical as well as the theoretical justification for the problem(s) under investigation. An important part of any thesis is a section on the significance of the study. Therefore, this question should be considered early in the life of a study.

At various key stages in planning a thesis, the feasibility of conducting a study must be faced. Hard questions should be asked about the resources needed for tackling a particular problem, and the justification in terms of time, effort and expense.

Determining the Thesis

A thesis is not the same as a topic to be investigated. While a topic may be particular crystals or the novels of Miles Franklin, a thesis is a statement that says, for instance, something about crystals or an author's novels. The distinction is important since in many ways the statement of a thesis determines the approach and stance writers take towards their topics or research questions.

A thesis is an idea or theory that is expressed as a statement, a contention for which evidence is gathered and discussed logically. The statement nearly always begins with the word *that*:

It is his thesis *that* the move towards republicanism in Australia began at the end of the last century.

The book's main thesis was *that* punishment of misdemeanours in school builds up feelings of resentment that impair learning.

A thesis is a sustained argument. The thesis statement usually appears in the first chapter where the background to the study is described; it will often determine the framework for the literature review and the data collection; and it is revisited in the final chapter. It permeates the whole study.

Reviewing the Literature

The review of literature is a task that continues throughout the duration of a thesis. It begins with a search for a suitable topic. Since a thesis aims to be a contribution to knowledge, a careful check should be made that the proposed study has not previously been undertaken. Although completely new and original problems are rare, a previous study should not be exactly replicated unless the techniques used were faulty, or the findings and conclusions doubtful, or unless some new sources of information have been discovered to provide information about the problem. A good test is whether the problem still requires solution.

Once a topic has been decided upon, it is essential to review all relevant material that has a bearing on the topic. This review of the literature is included in the final written thesis as a key section or chapter. It is necessary to show how the problem under investigation relates to previous research studies. In some subject areas it is important to locate the problem within a theoretical framework and, in such cases, the underlying theory needs to be reviewed as well.

In surveying a field initially, it is useful to work from the general to the specific, or from tertiary and secondary sources of information to primary sources.

Primary Sources

Primary sources of information include first-hand accounts of experimentation and investigation (articles in professional journals, monographs, doctoral theses, interviews and questionnaires), original works (letters, diaries, eyewitness accounts, poems, novels, autobiographies) and reports (proceedings of Parliament, court testimony, reports of government departments and agencies, annual reports, minutes).

Secondary Sources

Secondary sources of information are summaries of information gathered from primary sources. These include translations, summaries and reviews of research (for example, encyclopedia articles), abstracts, guide books and other publications containing information, commentaries, and so on.

Tertiary Sources

Textbooks are usually examples of tertiary sources of information, since these are generally compiled from secondary sources. Tertiary sources of information can be useful in providing an overview or broad summary of a field. They may even be acceptable as references because some textbooks become acknowledged as authorities. For certain types of research, the original source material may be lost or inaccessible and heavy reliance therefore must be made on secondary sources. However, there is no substitute for consulting primary sources if they are available, and postgraduate work in most subject areas demands it.

The reliability of sources of information generally decreases as the number of hands through which the information has passed increases.

The suggestions made in Chapter 2 for preparing a working bibliography and taking notes apply as much to the postgraduate thesis as to the undergraduate term paper. The use of cards for recording references and for taking notes is a widely accepted practice because of its efficiency.

Designing the Study

Choosing a design for a study essentially involves selecting the most appropriate methods or techniques to solve the particular problem under investigation. It is a crucial step in a thesis because, if a wrong decision is made, the whole study may be criticised on the grounds of inappropriate design or, even worse, as being unscientific or illogical.

It is difficult to generalise about research designs because of the wide variety of types of research. One subdivision is according to whether the approach is predominantly *quantitative* or *qualitative*. Quantitative research is typified by experimental studies in science based disciplines where findings are usually expressed in numerical form. Qualitative research, on the other hand, is characterised by ethnographic and historical studies where findings are more commonly expressed in words than in numbers.

Elements of Quantitative Studies

Certain elements of research design are common to both quantitative and qualitative studies, though in each case the interpretation of these elements may differ slightly. Other elements apply more appropriately to one or other of the broad approaches to research. The following elements are features of quantitative studies.

Statement of Hypotheses

In quantitative studies, research questions are usually re-expressed in terms of specific hypotheses to be tested. Hypotheses should be clearly stated and the relationship to previous research made clear. For the purpose of statistical testing, hypotheses may be expressed in the *null* form (e.g. *There is no difference between . . .*; or *There is no relationship between . . .*).

Statement of Assumptions

In every study, it is necessary to make certain assumptions. Wherever these are made, they should be stated clearly. Nothing should be taken for granted.

Statement of the Limitations of the Study

The time allowed for a study and restrictions of length in reporting it usually impose limitations on a study. Other limitations may be lack of subjects or equipment, or difficulty in accessing particular resources. These kinds of limitations need to be clearly stated.

Delimiting the Study

Delimitations, not to be confused with limitations, refer to ways in which the investigation has been reduced in size to make it manageable. A study may, for example, be delimited by investigating certain effects at particular levels or with particular age groups. Almost every study requires some focusing and how this is done needs to be stated.

Definition of Terms

All key terms and variables should be defined. The interpretation of the findings of a study depends in part on the way major variables are defined. For example, the statement that 'the incidence of juvenile delinquency was 23 per cent of all crimes' depends for its meaning on the definition of juvenile delinquency as well as the definition of crimes. Variables, then, need to be defined operationally in terms of how they are measured in quantifiable form.

Appropriateness of Research Design

The statistical methods for testing hypotheses need to be described and justified. Why was a particular statistical test selected? Will its application lead to the acceptance or rejection of hypotheses as stated? Significance levels for rejecting the null hypothesis need to be stated before applying statistical tests.

Description of Population and Sample

Most empirical or experimental studies require a random or representative sample to be drawn from some population. Questions to consider are whether the population and sample are adequately described and whether the method of sampling is appropriate. A basic concern in most studies is to guard against a biased sample. Considerable care needs to be exercised (and shown to be exercised) to guard against bias.

The Control of Error

The control of error is a key factor in experimental studies. The researcher conducting an experiment has to consider what variables are operating in a given situation. In the laboratory it is usually possible to control major variables or sources of error. For field studies it is usually only possible to control key variables, and researchers endeavour to randomise all others. In both cases, the variables and their control need to be described.

Reliability and Validity

In empirical studies it is necessary to establish the reliability and validity of test instruments. That is, do tests provide consistent measurements (a key aspect of reliability), and do tests measure what is claimed for them (a key aspect of validity)?

It cannot be emphasised too strongly that details of research design should be decided (and, preferably, written down) before the collection of data. The method of collecting data is often dictated by the research design. Indeed, most institutions require the submission of a formal written research proposal that must be approved before the student is permitted to undertake the study.

Elements of Qualitative Studies

Qualitative research stresses meanings in context rather than numerically measured data. The following guidelines refer predominantly to qualitative research in those disciplines or parts of disciplines that utilise such methods as case studies, questionnaire surveys, personal interviews and participant observation.

Statement of Hypotheses

The qualitative study employs the term *hypotheses* in a broader sense than empirical research. Instead, a particular argument or thesis is pursued. The qualitative researcher often begins by defining rather general concepts that, as research progresses, are tested, developed and often modified. Thus, there is need for some flexibility about an originally proposed hypothesis. All of this information needs to be clearly stated at the outset, along with how the work relates to previous research and the grounds for the choice of area researched.

Statement of Assumptions

As happens with all studies, certain assumptions are made which must be stated clearly so that there is no confusion as to the premises adopted. In studies where aspects of the social world are being explored, the researcher will also have cultural assumptions about various social groups or situations. While unavoidable, these must be kept in check so that personal bias does not endanger the credibility and integrity of the researcher. There are situations, however, where researchers can make known their personal values and state where they have called upon these to aid in interpreting data.

Limitations of the Study

Limitations of time, money and length of a study apply to all investigations, but the interpretive nature of qualitative research introduces a specific problem. One researcher's interpretations can often reasonably be challenged from quite a different perspective or within the context of a different historical period. This limitation must be kept in mind and formally acknowledged.

Delimitations

The topic of research must be focused to a manageable size and this usually requires reducing either the number of subjects or the time involved. Field researchers, in particular, often face the dilemma of knowing when to stop collecting data to prevent overload. Careful judgment is required to realise when sufficient information has been gathered to answer all initial and subsequent questions that have been posed.

Definition of Terms and Concepts

All key terms should be defined and stated clearly. The essence of some concepts, however, may change over the course of a research study, and so updated definitions or reclassifications of these are necessary. As an example of this, a researcher might start out with a notion that the average amount of housework done by a husband is thirty per cent of total shared duties, but after investigating might conclude that the average amount is closer to twenty per cent. The word *average* has changed and so needs reclassification.

Appropriateness of Research Design

In contrast to the empirical study whose main aim is the rejection or retention of a stated hypothesis, the qualitative study questions and interprets the meanings of the data in relation to the initial presuppositions and methods used. If the findings are then unsatisfactory or inconsistent, the structure of the study might need to be reassessed and corrective measures taken. For example, survey questionnaires have to be structured in such a way as to elicit the most useful responses. Closed questions (those with fixed responses) and open questions (no fixed responses) can be suitable for different types of research, and the advantages or disadvantages of each must be weighed up and justified.

Description of Population and Sample

While many studies require a random or representative sample to be drawn from a population, care must be taken to describe the method by which the sample was chosen and to ensure its appropriateness.

Much social research employs the process of theoretical sampling whereby the choice of subjects is guided by the researcher's developing theory, thus making it impossible to select all subjects in advance. This is because the researcher waits to see what the initial findings reveal before selecting further participants.

In the case of analytical case studies, research is usually carried out on a very small sample but in great detail and possibly for extended periods of time (sometimes years). Rather than requiring statistical generalisability from the findings, the issue here is more about recognising significant patterns and recurring themes within the context of a natural setting, which can then become catalysts for further research. The need to monitor consistently for undue bias is particularly crucial as case studies involve much researcher participation such as personal interviews and even lifestyle interaction.

The Control of Error

The concept of error is different from laboratory experiments since variables are prone to much less control and so need to be taken account of and described. Results are less concerned with statistical accuracy than with emerging concepts and categories that propel the researcher continually to test and update theory. Of course, there is always danger of error in the sense that a researcher's personal bias can interfere with suitable interpretation.

Reliability and Validity

It is as important in qualitative research as it is in quantitative research to evaluate data to ensure that the most effective methods are employed in data collection, and that the data directly address the questions posed at the outset. The methods should be determined before research begins, and most institutions require this information formally, for approval before research commences.

Qualitative researchers, while not relying on scientific measuring apparatus, must demonstrate reliability and validity by different means. Their credibility is confirmed to the extent that data are collected ethically, that any personal biases are kept in check, and that interpretations are sound. Because of the interpretive nature of the work, replication is not the issue that it is in scientific experiments and often replication is virtually impossible.

Interpreting the Data

Once data are collected, the qualitative researcher must be able to interpret these reliably. This process can involve summarising the data to a temporarily manageable length to categorise, identify themes, analyse and assess. From here, the researcher must look for meanings within the data and often relate findings to previous studies to see if these support existing research. If the findings seem to be in total opposition to the majority of other well-conducted studies in the field, the interpretation may have to be reassessed or the data collection process examined.

The main danger in interpretive data analysis is that interpretation is a personal process and researchers must be careful to distance themselves to a certain extent. It is also important that researchers do not over-generalise from small scale studies.

Combining Qualitative and Quantitative Research

It is sometimes desirable to combine qualitative with quantitative research to maximise the theoretical implications of research findings. Although this may be frowned upon by some because of the vastly different theoretical backgrounds and methods of data collection in the two approaches, a combined approach can prove valuable in certain projects.

Such a case is where objectively measured variables may be further clarified in ways that interpretive qualitative research can best offer. The reverse case applies when qualitative research findings can be used as a basis for future empirical research in the interests of expansion, explanation or support. Practical problems can arise, however, and the researcher must be extremely cautious to combine methods only if it is appropriate and if it ultimately leads to a greater understanding of underlying issues.

Plagiarism and Intellectual Property

In Chapter 2 the problem of plagiarism was noted. Good scholars always acknowledge their indebtedness to others by appropriate referencing. Another form of plagiarism to guard against may arise in the context of the relationship between the postgraduate student and the supervisor, where plagiarism may include false or misleading claims of ownership of what is termed *intellectual property.*

During a research project, students receive guidance, criticism and suggestions from supervisors. What students must avoid is inadvertently presenting any of a supervisor's original material as their own. The supervisor, too, has a responsibility not to contribute too much to a student's work, such as rewriting large sections; this can be a temptation in that a supervisor's professional status is enhanced through their successful students' achievements.

Likewise, students must take care to protect their own intellectual property. It might seem unthinkable for supervisors to pass off theories, hypotheses and findings arising from a student's work as their own but it does happen, although rarely. If any question of joint authorship arises – and it is standard practice in some of the science disciplines – it must be agreed upon by both student and supervisor. Further, it must not infringe on the originality of the student's completed work.

The above cases are difficult to regulate and monitor. Therefore, it is left to the integrity and ethical standards of both parties to ensure honest, professional conduct.

The Chapter Outline

The preparation of a chapter outline is a useful first step in writing the rough draft. The chapters in most theses and dissertations follow a fairly standard format. There is an introductory chapter and usually a chapter reviewing previous research. The next few chapters, the body of the thesis, vary according to the study. The empirical research study frequently has one or more chapters on procedures and techniques (hypotheses, sample, tests, research design) and one or more chapters on results of the study. The analytical research study frequently has a division of chapters according to a chronological development (for instance, early Stone Age, middle Stone Age, late Stone Age; the early years, the formative years, and so on) or some other clustering (perhaps poetry, drama, fiction, satire). The final chapter is for conclusions, implications of a theoretical or practical kind, recommendations where appropriate, and the need (if any) for further research.

Within each chapter there are major subheadings and there are minor subheadings. These headings often derive from the headings used in note taking or from some of the points described in this chapter (e.g. limitations, delimitations and significance of the study). A typical chapter outline for an introduction and a final chapter is shown in Figure 3.1.

---

1   INTRODUCTION
    Background to the Investigation
    Key Research Questions
    Significance of Study
    Setting of Study
    Limitations and Delimitations of the Study

                    *   *   *

7   CONCLUSIONS
    Recapitulation and Discussion
    Implications for Practice and Research
    A Direction for Future Research

Figure 3.1 Sample chapter outline for introduction and final chapter

A chapter outline is a guide for planning the thesis. Many headings will certainly change as the report progresses. The final form is determined by the nature of the study itself and by the conventions of scholarly writing.

Viewpoints of Examiners

Examiners are among the first readers of a thesis and it is instructive to consider their comments on previous theses. Figure 3.2 includes excerpts from examiners' reports where the problem or research questions under investigation are considered to be clearly stated. The examiners' comments included in Figure 3.3, on the other hand, indicate that the problem or research questions are vague or ill-defined. These comments make it quite clear that examiners look for, and peruse closely, the statement of aims and purposes.

The problem is well defined and clearly presented. ... Overall, Chapter 1 sets the scene for the study.

For a Master's dissertation, the work is outstanding. Particularly pleasing are parts of the second chapter where she laid the ground for her research focus. The rationale was discussed ably and clearly, and the theoretical justification for the research questions was fully established.

The research questions that the candidate raised, and the central problem, which activated those questions ... constitute central issues in the Australian educational context.

The aims of the study are particularly clearly set out and recognition of the limitations is good.

Chapter 1 provides a succinct delineation of the problem.

Problem Statement – The purposes of the study are succinctly outlined on p. 20 and are immediately followed by a listing of the research questions.

The fundamental purpose of the investigation is both an interesting and an important one.

Figure 3.2 Excerpts from examiners' reports indicating problem/research questions are clearly stated

I thought that the problem under investigation was left undefined and vague for too long. In the first paragraph the candidate states that the aim is to 'explore some aspects' of the school community relationship and it is not elaborated beyond this level until page 23 when the field study is discussed. Gradually the aim emerged as one read the thesis, but it needed to be much more explicit earlier in the study.

It is my impression that the difficulty in focusing and disciplining his thinking carried over to the methodology itself. I think the thesis would have been strengthened considerably if he had been able to develop some specific hypotheses around which he could have organised his methodology rather than approaching the subject from the standpoint of broad questions.

p. 9   Research question 3 is too vague to be meaningful.
        What sort of relationship?

The second observation relates to a fundamental weakness which flows through the thesis as a whole. Neither in the Summary nor the Introduction is there a clear statement indicating the author's central concern(s) or argument(s). The central question to be examined and the essential problems relating to them are not made explicit. This is most unfortunate because large sections of the thesis provide most valuable and important information and analysis (e.g. in Chapters 2, 4 & 5) but they are not generally related to a central theme and the thesis therefore tends to be rather episodic and at times disjointed.

Questions 1–6 are far too broad to answer with this study. The underlying assumption is interesting — that an aptitude is a composite of abilities — but controversial.

Figure 3.3 Excerpts from examiners' reports indicating problem/research questions are vague and ill-defined

This chapter highlights the importance of stating one's thesis clearly. It is imperative that readers understand what is the purpose of a study. Therefore, a statement of the major aims and purposes of an investigation will generally feature prominently in the opening chapter; there may be a restatement or reformulation in a later chapter in the light of a review of previous work in the field; and the aims may be returned to in the final concluding chapter.

Chapter

SCHOLARLY WRITING:
A CASE STUDY

In an article titled 'The research paper: time and technique'[1], Professor Pauk recounts one student's experiences of writing a term paper. Although the scene is set in another continent, the issues raised are pertinent in universities and other educational institutions everywhere.

* * *

Registration was like a game of chess. The smart students made their moves early. Some lined up before dawn, while others used the university's new computerized system to register from home by telephone. They registered early, not especially to get the best courses, but to avoid being 'stuck' with one — the one taught by Professor Wilbur Hendricon.

The word on the grapevine was that this was a course to be avoided by the faint of heart. The chances of being forced into Professor Hendricon's course were slim but still too terrifying to take a chance. Professor Hendricon had, as the students said, 'a special deal with the administration.' He could hand-pick twenty-five students for his class, but had to take another ten at general registration.

This unusual procedure was a compromise. It came about this way: Professor Hendricon had taught only graduate courses before; but ten years ago he decided that he would like to teach one section of English 105. So Professor Hendricon suddenly proclaimed to the dean that he would take twenty-five first-year students and turn them into scholars.

The dean was faced with a dilemma. On the one hand, a negative answer might be taken as a rude rebuff by the proud and sensitive Hendricon. Also,

---

1. W. Pauk, *How to Study in College*, 5th edn. Copyright 1993 by Houghton Mifflin Company. Reprinted with permission. Adapted from the article originally published as 'The research paper: time and technique' in the *Journal of Reading*, October 1969. Copyright 1969 Walter Pauk and the International Reading Association. All rights reserved.

the dean thought, 'If he resigns, I will have to answer to the president.' Hendricon was the university's brilliant light and he was eagerly sought after by other universities. On the other hand, a positive answer would be a blow to the morale of the other members of the English Department, who had no choice but to take their usual thirty-five students per class. The dean consulted her colleagues and persuaded them to accept the compromise. Needless to say, I was one of the unlucky ten.

Right from the very first day in class, I could see how well Hendricon had chosen. The twenty-five were geniuses. I later discovered that they all had straight As in high school and that they were clustered at the top of the scholarship list. Furthermore, they exelled in language and literature, while my strengths were in mathematics and music. Math skills and musical talent did not count for much in an English course.

At first I thought Professor Hendricon's legendary standards might just be rumor, but after the first test any hopes evaporated. We unfortunate ten compared notes and found our grades in the 30s and 40s. But no one questioned Professor Hendricon's honesty and sincerity. Our papers were filled with notations, symbols, and helpful comments. We did, however, question his standards. They were not for us mortals.

Six of the ten transferred to other sections of the course immediately; the other three students transferred after the second test. Everyone knew that transferring was possible. The other instructors expected to get all ten of us in their classes within the first few weeks of term. In this way morale was preserved, because administratively, at least, all the classes started out with thirty-five students each.

Perhaps it was the lemming instinct in me or perhaps it was Hendricon's appeal, but I decided to hang in. On the day after the last date for changing classes, I took my usual seat. The other twenty-five students, who usually chatted loudly until Professor Hendricon entered the door, were strangely silent today. You see, in all these past ten years, not one of the unchosen had ever stayed in Hendricon's class. Everyone knew this.

We could hear Hendricon's brisk but firm footsteps drawing closer to the open door. The pace was faster than usual. We saw the toe of his left foot puncture the blank space of the doorway. The blood was pounding in my temples. My breathing was fast and shallow. Hendricon always walked straight to the lectern, put down his notes, and said 'good afternoon' to the class. As he entered today, he glanced at me with a curious look. He did not greet the class as usual. He just lectured, but more seriously. I could not keep my mind on the lecture. No one could. It seemed that I had spoiled the atmosphere of this select club. Why had I not been less foolhardy?

On Monday, however, the class resumed its normal pace and atmosphere. I was present but not accepted. The chosen twenty-five sat in a solid square. I sat outside the square, separate but linked like an appendix. But that did not bother me, for I was really fascinated by Professor Hendricon. He was a great teacher. I took copious notes and studied the assignments carefully.

I occasionally forgot myself and spoke out during discussions. I worked hard on tests and examinations, but they were never quite up to standard. I could usually understand the ideas and concepts, but time always ran out. I needed more time to think. But I was not discouraged because I was enjoying the course and learning a lot.

It was just after the Christmas holidays that Professor Hendricon announced it. 'It' was the research paper — 3500 words and counting for one-third of the final grade. I should have been petrified because I could not write, and yet, I was glad. This was my chance to raise my present hard-earned average of 62.7% to the necessary 70.

This would be the first instance where I would have an advantage over the students — I would have the advantage of time. I needed time. Time is the great equalizer; time is democratic. We all receive the same amount of it every morning. No distinction is made between the genius and the plodder. This is what I told myself; it helped me feel a little better.

There should not have been any excitement because everyone knew about the Hendricon paper. It was indeed another factor that encouraged the rush to register early for other courses. The paper was not due until after the late winter break — almost two months off. But still, there were groans and whisperings. I could hardly hear the professor's caution against plagiarism. 'Use both the primary text as well as secondary critical sources,' he instructed against a background of restless inattention. Very few paid attention to his next point about thinking carefully before choosing a topic. I somehow caught, 'Once you have decided on your topic it should be narrowed three or four times.' What did he mean by this?

After the others had left, I edged up to Professor Hendricon, who was gathering up his lecture notes, and asked about the idea of narrowing the topic. He said, 'If, for example, you were doing a history course, and you chose as your topic the "Civil War," you would be almost sure to fail. You simply could not do justice to such a large topic — dozens of books would be necessary to cover that subject, not an undergraduate research paper. Even a second narrowing of the topic to the "Battle of Gettysburg," a major engagement in the war, would still be too broad. A third stage of narrowing such as the "Battle of Cemetery Ridge" would be more manageable, but your focus might not be sufficiently defined yet. So perhaps a further narrowing to the "Tactical Importance of Cemetery Ridge" might be necessary. This would be an aspect of the original broad topic on which adequate information could be found to write an in-depth paper.'

I was so excited about writing the term paper that I went straight to the library eager and determined to find an interesting topic on which to use this technique of narrowing. I was surprised to find the cavernous library so empty of students. But of course, there would be time during 'reading week' and the late winter break — there was no pressure yet. I went directly to the reference librarian who showed me how to use the various special reference books. Another librarian, who joined us, had an interesting idea.

She said, 'If you choose a subject area carefully in your first year, and continue throughout your university years to research and write in that area, you could probably become quite an expert.' This idea intrigued me.

Over the next few days I brainstormed possible topics for my paper. First, I scrutinized Professor Hendricon's course outline, mulling over his lecture themes and the prescribed authors and texts. Then I returned to the library to peruse reference books such as encyclopedias, surveys of literature, and biographical dictionaries. I developed a list of nineteen topics that interested me. I reflected on these over the weekend and after careful deliberation rejected fourteen of them.

The remaining five topics I decided to discuss with Professor Hendricon. He seemed happy to see me. In about five minutes we eliminated two. As far as the other three were concerned, he suggested that I talk about each with professors who were experts in the respective areas.

These talks were especially stimulating. I got to know three new professors from whom I received not only useful insights about narrowing the topics but also details of important sources and prominent authorities as well. After thinking through the suggestions made by these professors. I settled on the area that was most appealing to me.

I arranged another session with Professor Hendricon to inform him of my decision and to obtain advice on the direction my assignment should take. We discussed the precise purpose of my paper, and, over a cup of tea, we juggled words and finally formulated a challenging question to launch my research. I emerged from his Dickensian study aglow with inspiration and enthusiasm. The stern and serious Hendricon of the lecture hall had a warm and sensitive side that few students had glimpsed.

So, with the topic narrowed and a clear sense of direction established, back to the library I went to search for sources and to start my research. With the first week over I was surprised to find none of the class in the library. During the first term I had learned how to use the library's computerized catalogue. Why not explore other searching opportunities offered by the computer system, such as using a key word to locate titles relevant to the focus of my research? I was amazed at the wealth of material available through the computer catalogue, and soon I had an impressive list of titles in my working bibliography. Gaining confidence, I decided to use the CD-ROM databases and discovered a number of periodical articles pertaining to my research question.

I gathered some of my sources and began taking notes on pages of paper. The reference librarian, ever helpful, wandered over and asked if I knew the advantages of recording my notes on 3 × 5 slips. Without waiting for an answer, she said that the ability to categorize my notes would ensure a much more efficient research system. Her specific suggestions were these:

- Record only one point, or a small cluster of related points, on one card.
- Record only information that is relevant to the purpose of the research.
- Use only one side of the card.

- Each card should indicate the author and page numbers of the source.
- Enclose all verbatim notes in quotation marks.
- Most notes should be paraphrased or summarized.
- Whenever you have a thought or insight of your own, jot it down and enclose it with brackets to signify 'my own'.

Noticing that I had no slips, she darted to her desk and pulled out the bottom drawer and thumped several rubber-banded stacks of cards on my table. 'These are old cards left over when we converted the catalogue to a computer system. They are only used on one side. You are welcome to use them for your research notes.'

The card method intrigued me and now that I had a wide-ranging list of sources, I was anxious to get started on the research. I worked steadily in the library for the next two weeks, averaging two or three hours a day. It was surprisingly easy jotting down important information and ideas on cards and indicating the sources and page numbers. Rather than wasting time writing out the author's name or the title on each card, I used a simple coding system to identify each source. I did not have a written outline. I had tried to prepare one after formulating my question, but I could not anticipate the material I would find. I also sensed that it would be too restricting. However, although I did not have an outline, it would be unfair to say that I selected the material for my note cards haphazardly. I selected material that had a bearing on my specific question. Once I immersed myself in the research, I began to sense what was relevant and what was not.

After two weeks, I had a shoebox full of cards. I was ready to start structuring and drafting the paper. During the course of the research I had sketched out a tentative list of sections that might serve as an outline. I stepped back from my intense two-week spell of research to reflect on the provisional outline. Keeping the research question uppermost in my mind, I modified the sections so that they would provide a structure around which I could shape my answer. Next, I read through all my note cards and moved them into categories corresponding to my outline. Having notes on each card that pertained to only one idea permitted me to place the cards in separate categories. If I had put two different notes on one card, I would have had to rewrite the information onto two separate cards now. I was glad that I had a system. It was like playing cards.

My outline required further modification because not all the cards fitted the major sections. I added another section to accommodate some of the cards, while a number of cards simply did not fit into any of the sections. So, with the cards in categories, I started to follow the second step of the librarian's advice. I began to shift the piles of cards into an order that seemed logical for my paper. It was surprisingly easy to re-order the piles of cards so that there was a logical flow in the sequence of the sections.

With the categories of cards spread out before me, I began to study each category independently to create a detailed outline. As I wrestled with sections, subsections and supporting material I began to see where I had gaps in data and weak spots in the argument. My detailed outline revealed plainly the areas in which my paper lacked balance and completeness. My work was cut out for the next few days since I needed specifics that the paper presently lacked. I was glad that each card carried a reference to the source, so that I could locate not only the source but the precise page as well.

After a few hours of additional research in the library, I was able to augment my note cards. I felt that the more complete I could make my collection of cards, the more effective the first draft would be. I remembered Professor Hendricon's advice: 'If you do not gather enough first-class material, you will have trouble writing a major paper.' I used some of the new research information to revise and refine my detailed outline.

Finally, I was satisfied with my outline. Then I began to write the first draft. It surprised me to see how easy it is to write a long paper once the material is placed in order. I actually enjoyed the process. It took four days of writing in my spare time to complete the draft. I preferred writing my first draft in longhand because I seemed to think more clearly when writing rather than typing. On each day, I concentrated on writing one of four major parts of the paper. When I had finished, I immediately read it over and it sounded good to me — so good that I knew I would be able to enjoy the late-winter holidays. A wonderful reward. First, I had to type up my draft on the computer, and after saving it carefully on the hard drive, I took the floppy disk over to the computer center and printed a copy. I proudly left the copy on my desk to cool while I went home for the holidays.

On the last day before we departed for our week's holiday, Professor Hendricon did his duty as a teacher to remind us to work on our papers because they were due five days after our return to campus. The students fidgeted, a nervous laugh or two mingled with some of the spontaneous whispering, but no one said anything. I thought to myself that I had not seen any of the chosen twenty-five in the library; but then they could have been there at other times. Also, the thought struck me that they loved to discuss every moot point and debate hypothetical issues. They seemed to excel at writing creative papers, often at the last minute, with information they already had in their heads. Perhaps a research paper that demanded hard and dogged work was just too rigorous for their creative souls. Well, I just thought these thoughts and was a bit ashamed at my suspicious mind.

Even though I was still failing Professor Hendricon's course, the warm feeling generated by my completed draft provided the tone that I needed to enjoy my holidays. I had a good rest.

I arrived back on campus on Friday to avoid the weekend traffic. That evening, feeling proud of myself, I casually picked up my draft and, to extract the maximum amount of satisfaction from my accomplishment, I began reading. By the time I had finished page 3, my smile had vanished, and by page 10 fear had gripped me. The development of my thesis, which sounded so smooth upon completion, was now disjointed and repetitious and some paragraphs were meaningless. How could that be?

I pacified myself after the initial shock by realizing that I still had seven days, while many of the other students in the class had not even started their papers. Most of them would only arrive back on campus on Sunday evening, and that would leave them but a scant five days. As I pondered how to fix up my research paper, I realized, for the first time, the truth of the words which I had discarded as 'teachers' preachings': 'No paper should ever be handed in unless you have revised it. For the revision to be effective, you must always put your paper away for a few days so that you will lose some familiarity with it. Then, when you reread it, you will be better able to spot the weaknesses and the rough sections. Once these are spotted, revise, revise, revise.'

My paper was certainly rough. I recalled the steps for revising; first look through the draft to make sure the ideas are understandable and supported by details and examples. Second, make sure the organizational plan for the paper is clear and that the sections are in logical sequence. Third, check for consistency of style, and, finally, ensure that the mechanics such as spelling and hyphenating are correct. I discovered that I had scattered throughout the paper bits of interesting information — interesting but not always pertinent. I added some of the misplaced material to the introduction and eliminated the rest. It was tough to throw away these gems that I had worked so hard to extract from my sources, but I heard ringing in my ears: 'Good writers don't put everything down that is interesting. Remember the iceberg with its nine-tenths underwater and only one-tenth showing above the surface. This submerged part — your background work — gives the iceberg its strength and power.'

After weeding out the irrelevant material, I concentrated on the structure of the paper and discovered that it, too, was a bit vague. Parts of the general statement that should have been at the beginning were in the body of the paper. So I sharpened the introduction by stating the thesis and then broke it down to the five main points that I had planned to establish and support. By the time I had reworked the introduction, I really knew for the first time what I was attempting to do. I was shocked to realize that my own understanding of what I was trying to do had not been clear. By the time I went to sleep on Sunday, I had hammered out a clear statement of what I was trying to establish and support.

Monday rolled around all too soon. The vacation was over. There was a lot of activity on campus as students accelerated into a faster tempo of study. Papers were due, final examinations hovered on the horizon, and most plans to complete work during the holidays had fallen through. Hendricon reminded the class of the Friday deadline. There was no whispering this time, just grim silence. I, too, contributed to the silence. I had to write not only a passing paper, but a paper good enough to earn an 85 if I was to raise my average to the passing grade of 70. I had, perhaps, counted too heavily on time and technique. Time was running out and technique was not holding up. But I still had a chance. Most of the chosen twenty-five, I was sure, had not even started.

I worked hard to strengthen the body of the paper by realigning my main sections in the same order as in the statement of thesis in the introduction. I made sure that each main section led off with a brief paragraph that introduced the section. Then I grouped the supporting information in a number of separate paragraphs all focused on the central idea of the section. As I worked through the other sections checking the paragraph structure, I was surprised to discover that some of the supporting materials were still widely scattered even though I had carefully laid out a sequence when I grouped my note cards. By moving some of the information to more appropriate sections, I was able to eliminate repetition. I reworked each main section, especially those that seemed vague or hastily composed. Occasionally, I dug back into my collection of note cards when an idea needed additional support.

On Tuesday I fashioned a concluding summary that was not repetitious, synthesizing the thesis and key points in such a way [as] to show mastery of the material. After dinner I took my disk over to the computer center and printed a copy of the complete paper. I was immensely relieved and satisfied when I fell asleep that evening.

After the 9 o'clock class on Wednesday, I was free to devote the whole day to the final editing of the essay. I first read the entire paper aloud, checking for style. By reading aloud I could better detect redundant words, vague phrases, and awkward sounding sentences. I corrected the flawed sentences so that they flowed smoothly and naturally. As part of the editing process, I made frequent use of a dictionary and a thesaurus to ensure that the vocabulary was precise. Also, I worked on internal transitions to give my paragraphs and sentences better cohesion. After I had edited the printed copy, I corrected the computer version and saved it carefully. I was meticulous in backing up copies on diskette in the event my computer malfunctioned.

I woke early on Thursday excited to see the final copy in print at last. I rushed down to the computer room after breakfast and printed out my 'magnum opus.' I was so anxious to start proofreading that I toyed with the possibility of skipping my morning lectures. But with final examinations looming, common sense won out! After lectures, I gobbled my lunch down and headed for my room and my prized paper. I proofread it meticulously, from title page to bibliography. All my thoroughness had paid off — not a single error was apparent. I was flushed with that warm feeling of satisfaction that the completion of a creative assignment brings.

This was it. This was the day! I never heard such an outpouring of incidents to a professor from frantic, frightened students who tried so hard to look and act sophisticated. 'The library is so full, you can't find a table to write on.' 'Two other students are working on the same topic as I am and I cannot get hold of the sources.' 'My computer crashed.' 'My printer overheated and seized up.' 'I'll need more time, because all the typists in town are busy, and they can't get to mine until after the weekend.'

Hendricon was calm but exceedingly serious. He looked around the room solemnly, making no attempt to answer any of the excuses. After a moment, he held up his hand for quiet and went on with his lecture as if nothing had happened. There was deep silence that hour. Professor Hendricon was always good, but he was especially good that day. He talked hard and earnestly. Most of the students sat glumly, motionless and glassy-eyed. Only a few had the discipline to take notes. For some reason, the professor's words seemed to be aimed at me. He was trying to make scholars of us, as well as mature men and women. About half the students handed in papers that day. Spurred by the announcement, 'Five points a day will be deducted on all late papers,' the rest were in on the following Monday. I was pleased and proud that mine was in on time.

With only two and a half weeks to go, Professor Hendricon lectured hard and fast, determined to complete his schedule of lectures. By now, I had reconciled myself that failure was a possibility. Though I still wanted to pass the course, I was not too worried about it. I was just glad to have had the opportunity to attend Professor Hendricon's class.

On the last day of class, Professor Hendricon strode in with our research papers. 'Before I hand them back to you,' he said, 'I want to talk about them both generally and specifically.' He continued, 'A few of the papers were excellent, a few poor, and the majority mediocre. The excellent ones were creative and imaginative in their use of technique; but the poor ones seemed as if they had been put together artificially and mechanically with scissors and paste.'

That last remark hit me. Of course, I should have known that Professor Hendricon would be quick to see the artificial way my paper was put together: how I took notes on cards; distributed them in piles; mechanically shifted stacks of cards around; made an outline last, not first; filled gaps by digging out more material; mechanically revising, looking up words, reading aloud to detect faulty intonation — all done like a 'hack' in mechanical and piecemeal fashion. The rest of the class had real talent — they were truly gifted. In four or five days, they were able to write down their thoughts directly, fully developed, like true artists. And like true artists, they made good with one chance, whereas I had dozens of chances to write and rewrite.

As Professor Hendricon continued to talk about 'scissors and paste,' he suddenly picked up a paper to illustrate a point. I was shocked. I could tell it was my paper. I just couldn't stand the embarrassment. All I wanted to do was to get out of that room, fast! Then I suddenly realized that though I knew it was my paper, no one else did. So I steeled myself. Professor Henricon read one paragraph after another. He jumped to the first part of the paper for a paragraph, then to the end for another. Then I noticed that the rest of the class was listening attentively, and though Professor Hendricon's voice was excited, it was kindly. As I calmed and composed myself, I heard, 'Note the smooth rhythm of the prose and the careful choice of words. This is what I mean by scholarship. The technique is discernible. Yes! But put together with a scholar's love, and care, and time.'

P.S. You guessed it. I passed the course.

Chapter 5

COMPUTER TOOLS
FOR WRITING

Students at all levels find that the computer not only makes them more productive but is fast becoming indispensable for writing and research. Foremost among computer software tools are word processors. Further useful text tools include spelling checkers, thesauri and even programs to check grammar and analyse style. Available also are publishing and printing tools, management and presentation tools. These, and other tools for scanning, can help in different facets of assignment and thesis writing. Of course, term papers and even theses will continue to be produced with the older technologies of pen and typewriter, but newer computer-based technologies are making available exciting planning and organisational tools. Students not familiar with these can handicap themselves.

This chapter describes the range of writing and research tools ushered in by the computer as well as how these can help with many aspects of assignment and thesis writing.

Text Tools

What transforms the desktop, laptop or notebook computer into a versatile writing tool are application programs or software. One does not need to be a programmer to use such programs although a familiarity with computers is helpful (loading programs and saving documents, for example), as is knowing how a particular program works (for instance, to centre headings or indent text). This section provides a brief introduction to the most important text tool of all — word processors. There follows a brief note of other writing aids such as spelling checkers, thesauri, grammar checkers, and style analysers.

Word Processors

A word processor is an application program that is acquired for running on a particular computer. There are scores of word processors on the market, designed for different kinds of computers and offering a variety of functions or features. A word processor is like a typewriter in that it enables one to type and display text on a page. However, because word processors work electronically rather than manually, text is *stored*, which means it can subsequently be retrieved, amended, added to, and arranged in different ways before printing. Thus revision of writing becomes far less of a chore, even enjoyable. Furthermore, lecturers and thesis supervisors can be presented with drafts that are easy to read. Students, too, can work on printed copies, and many writers still prefer to do their finer editing on paper. The added bonus is that much of the worry about losing drafts is removed since back-up copies of all writing can be made easily on disk or paper.

All word processing programs perform a range of general tasks in ways that are not too dissimilar, with the result that having learned to use one word processor it is generally straightforward to switch to another. Where word processors differ is in ease of use and number of features offered (which in turn affects price). If looking to purchase a word processor, first find processors that run on the type of computer you intend to use and, next, determine what are essential and desirable features for the writing demands of a particular subject or field.

Text is generally entered at a keyboard, though for some purposes text may be scanned (see *Scanners*, page 51). Many writers soon become sufficiently familiar with computers to compose at the keyboard, thus achieving enormous savings of time.

The *word wrap* feature of word processors allows one to concentrate on writing without regard to length of line – if a word does not fit on a line within the margins set, it automatically wraps around to the next line. Other features common to most word processors allow one to position a cursor or pointer within text to insert or delete portions, or to cut parts and copy these to other sections (termed *cut*, *copy*, and *paste*). An *undo* function is useful to reverse an editing function that was not intended or which had unexpected consequences.

Search and *replace* are other functions common to most word processors. The search function allows particular text to be located (useful in a long document) while the search and replace functions in combination allow text to be changed, perhaps for consistency of spelling or form of citation.

A *save* function allows writing to be saved periodically. Some word processors save automatically after given periods of time or a certain number of keystrokes; or the user may be prompted to save regularly. The best advice for all computer users is to save often and to make regular back-ups of all writing. Making a back-up involves saving another copy on another disk or medium (and, sensibly, keeping the copy in a different place from the original). Disks are not indestructible and accidents do happen. However, saving is quick and should be done frequently.

Other functions of word processors fall into the category of formatting or arranging the appearance of text on a page. Here one must determine what functions are most useful or essential for particular kinds of writing.

The use of **boldface** or *italics* is one way that word processing documents differ from typewritten documents since previously most typewriters were limited to underlining or the use of capitals. The first edition of this book, written before the appearance of word processors, adopted the convention of underlining for book and journal titles and for certain categories of headings. The widespread use of word processing has changed this convention. Printed books rarely use underlining, adopting instead boldface or italics. Details are given in the chapters following. While most word processors allow text to be formatted in bold or italics, it is important to check that the printer to be used incorporates these enhancements (see *Printers*, page 51).

Other fairly standard formatting functions include:

- *setting of margins* allowing the user to set left and right margins (and so fix line length) and to set top and bottom margins
- *setting tabs* so that pressing the tab key indents the cursor to predefined positions
- *justification* permitting fully justified text as in the paragraphs above where lines are extended to the right margin giving straight edges on the right and the left
- *centring* to centre a heading or line
- *line spacing* for specifying the printing of text as single spaced, space and a half, or double spaced
- *page numbering* for automatic increments of page numbers through a document.

Other word processing features permit the use of various fonts (e.g. Times, Geneva, Bookman) and different point sizes (e.g. 12 point, 14 point, 18 point). The term WYSIWYG has been coined for those word processing programs where *what you see* (on screen) is *what you get* (when printed).

For some users, *superscripts* (e.g. $32°$) and subscripts (e.g. H_2SO_4) will be important features. Important for others will be the facility to include *statistical formulae* or *mathematical equations* in documents. For yet others, the use of *footnotes* or *endnotes* will be essential features. Where running heads or footers are desired to print items such as section or chapter titles at the top or bottom of pages, a program with a *headers* and *footers* facility will be sought. For writing where tabular information is common, a *tables* feature will be a valuable asset. Many other features (e.g. the use of glossaries, indexing, compiling tables of contents, kerning, hyphenation, multiple columns, nested indents) are included in larger, more professional (and usually more expensive) word processing programs.

The purpose of this section is to highlight those aspects of assignment and thesis writing where the use of a word processor takes account of many of the routine tasks of editing and formatting, allowing the writer then to focus on content.

Spelling Checkers

Spelling errors in written assignments or graduate theses mar the finished product and suggest a degree of carelessness. This is unfortunate because some errors may be typographic. Spelling errors can be difficult to locate when reading for meaning yet examiners nearly always seem to find some.

Help is at hand with spelling checkers, available sometimes as separate programs used in conjunction with a word processor or as part of a word processor itself. Such checkers work extremely fast, checking every word in a document against an in-built dictionary often containing 80,000 words or more. Whenever a mismatch is found, it is highlighted and, in the better spelling checkers, shown in context. Many spelling checkers may even include suggestions for correction. Some words may be shown as mismatches because they are technical words and not included in a particular dictionary. Users often have the option here to create their own user dictionaries to augment the in-built dictionary provided. In all cases, however, it is the writer who must decide what action to take for each mismatch — ignoring it, for instance in the case of technical words known to be correct, accepting one of the suggested changes, or checking the spelling in a reputable dictionary like the *Macquarie* and then making changes as necessary.

Spelling checkers are not foolproof. They will not detect *there*, for instance, as a mismatch when *their* was intended. Nor will they detect *t* as an error when *to* was intended since single letters of the alphabet are included in most dictionaries. However, spelling checkers usually detect 97–98 per cent of genuine spelling or typographical errors. A spelling checker is an extremely useful text tool.

Thesauri

When looking for just the right word to place in a phrase or sentence, most writers turn to a thesaurus such as that first produced by Roget in 1852. This first edition was titled *Thesaurus of English Words and Phrases, Classified and Arranged so as to Facilitate the Expression of Ideas and*

Assist in Literary Composition. Subsequent editions sold more than 30 million copies. Not surprisingly, thesauri are now available on computer, either as separate programs or as add-on modules to word processors. Look up the word *separate*, for instance, and one electronic thesaurus shows three meanings: the adjective *apart*, and two verbs *split* and *isolate* (see Figure 5.1). Synonyms for *apart*, the word highlighted, are given in the right column. To obtain synonyms for *isolate* or *split*, simply point to the word (that is, click with a mouse), and a list of synonyms is displayed in the right column.

Meanings For: separate	Synonyms:
apart (adj)	divided
split (verb)	individual
isolate (verb)	independent
Antonyms	unattached
	disconnected
	detached
	distinct

Figure 5.1 An electronic thesaurus displays different meanings for the word *separate* in the left column while in the right column are displayed synonyms for the word highlighted.

To find words opposite in meaning to *separate*, click on *Antonyms* to see a further scrolling list, part of which is shown in Figure 5.2.

Meanings For: separate	Antonyms:
apart (adj)	**attach**
split (verb)	blend
isolate (verb)	combine
Antonyms	conglomerate
	connect
	connected
	consolidate
	dependent
	fuse

Figure 5.2 To find antonyms for the word *separate* with the electronic thesaurus, users click on *Antonyms* and a scrolling list of antonyms is displayed immediately in the right column.

With some word processors, clicking on a synonym or antonym such as any of those shown in the right column of Figure 5.2 immediately places that word in the text.

A thesaurus, whether in book or electronic form, is without question a vital text tool for all writers.

Grammar Checkers

Writers also can check certain aspects of grammar and punctuation with grammar checkers which, like spelling checkers and thesauri, come as separate programs or as part of some word processors. Grammar checkers commonly flag such aspects as split infinitives, unbalanced quotation marks, repetition of words and commonly confused words.

As with spelling checkers, the writer decides what action to take in any instance: grammar checkers can simply point to what may be potential problems. Many of the problems may be of a relatively super-ficial kind but, nevertheless, here is another text tool that can usefully augment the other tools described in this section, all of which are readily available for those using personal computers for their assignment or thesis writing.

Style Analysers

Closely related to grammar checkers are style analysers that commonly check documents for use of clichés, wordy expressions, imprecise use of language, colloquialisms, non-standard expressions, and even words that may offend. Other style checks can include flagging of nominalisations and uses of the verb *to be* which often signal passive constructions. Some style analysers go beyond the word level and attempt to determine the organisation of sentences and paragraphs within a document.

Style analysers frequently include various counts and averages (number and length of words, average sentence length, and so on) and may even provide estimates of the overall reading difficulty of documents.

Some of these checks, counts and indexes will be more useful than others, or may be more useful at certain stages of writing. All are designed essentially to signal to authors what may be potential problems or stumbling blocks in writing.

Mathematical Symbols and Equations

Electronic tools for writing and printing mathematical symbols and equations are helpful especially for students in mathematics, physics and statistics. Specially designed mathematics word processors are available. Some general purpose word processors also incorporate functions for handling mathematical equations.

The examples in Figure 5.3 illustrate the kinds of mathematical expressions and equations produced using a word processor with an in-built equation editor. This editor spaces, sizes and positions all symbols according to the usual conventions for typesetting mathematical text. The user is then able to make fine adjustments as necessary.

$$\frac{\sigma^2_{\text{true}}}{\sigma^2_{\text{obs}}} = \frac{\sigma^2_p}{\sigma^2_p + \dfrac{\sigma^2_q}{n_q} + \dfrac{\sigma^2_r}{n_r} + \dfrac{\sigma^2_{pq}}{n_q} + \dfrac{\sigma^2_{pr}}{n_r} + \dfrac{\sigma^2_{qr}}{n_q n_r} + \dfrac{\sigma^2_{pqr}}{n_q n_r}} \tag{8}$$

$$\alpha = \frac{n}{n-1} \left(1 - \frac{\displaystyle\sum_{i=1}^{m} S_i^2}{S_x^2} \right) \tag{12}$$

$$\eta^2_{yx} = \frac{\displaystyle\sum_{i=1}^{n} m(\bar{y}_i - \bar{\bar{y}})^2}{\displaystyle\sum_{i=1}^{n}\sum_{j=1}^{m} (\bar{y}_{ij} - \bar{\bar{y}})^2}$$

$$\rho = \frac{\dfrac{SS_B}{n-1} - \dfrac{SS_w}{(n-1)(m-1)}}{\dfrac{SS_B}{n-1} + \dfrac{(m-1)SS_W}{(n-1)(m-1)}}$$

Figure 5.3 Mathematical expressions and equations produced by a word processor with an equation editor facility[†]

[†] Equations drawn from Keeves, J.P. (ed.) 1992. *The IEA Technical Handbook*. International Association for the Evaluation of Educational Achievement, The Hague.

Students whose writing involves considerable use of mathematical symbols and expressions will find an equation editor an essential tool.

Diacritical Marks and Other Special Characters

Students whose writing involves languages other than English will find useful a word processor that handles fonts containing diacritical marks (accent, circumflex, tilde and umlaut) for several of the European languages, or special fonts for languages with non-roman scripts. Indeed, all writers who refer to authors with non-English names will find these features an asset.

Diacritical marks contained in many fonts for word processors include:

é   acute accent
è   grave accent
î   circumflex
ñ   tilde
ü   umlaut

Other fonts contain the Greek and other alphabets as well as many special characters:

© ¿ £ # ¶ † « » ® ™ ≠ { | }

Students who know what features are available in different word processors are helped in matching a word processor to their particular writing needs.

Publishing and Printing Tools

The text tools described above are useful for writing and for the various stages of revision. Publishing and printing tools are discussed briefly in this section.

Desktop Publishing

Just as computers have dramatically changed the way people write using word processors, so have computers changed publishing. Desktop publishing refers to the use of personal computers to prepare text, often together with graphics, for printing on a high quality printer. Again, it is software that transforms the computer into a tool for desktop publishing.

Desktop publishing programs made their first appearance in the mid eighties; today there are desktop publishing programs that students in secondary and primary schools use for producing brochures, newsletters and school magazines. While most students submitting assignments and theses find a word processor sufficient for their purposes, such written projects commonly include graphs, figures and other art work. A desktop publishing program gives the user greater control in placing these on the page. Other desktop publishing features allow graphics to be scaled (useful for page placement) and for spacing between letters, called kerning, to be adjusted (useful for laying out of complex tables). Many features of desktop publishing programs are becoming available in top-of-the-market word processors and so the distinguishing line between these types of programs is quite blurred.

Printers

The overall appearance of an assignment or thesis utilising a word processor and other text tools, and perhaps a desktop publishing program, will depend ultimately on the quality of the printer. A poor printer attached to the best computer and software will produce a poor looking product. The content may be satisfactory but the presentation may detract.

Most frequently used with personal computers are dot-matrix printers, ink jet printers and laser printers. The quality of dot-matrix printers depends on the number of pins in the print head and the speed of printing. Using a slower speed results in near letter quality print approximating that of a good electric typewriter. Ink jet printers do not strike the paper as do dot-matrix printers and the result is quieter operation, much higher quality print, but slower operation. At the top of the range are laser printers that produce very high quality print and graphics, and quiet, relatively fast operation compared with both dot-matrix and ink jet printers.

When choosing a word processor and computer, it is not always appreciated that careful consideration needs to be given to a printer. Two obvious points to consider are: first, the printer needs to be compatible with the computer; and, second, the printer needs to be able to handle any formatting in a document such as the use of different fonts, and enhancements like boldface, italics, subscripts, superscripts and graphics.

Scanners

A scanner works much like a photocopier but the images and text captured are transformed into electronic images or text that may then be imported to a word processor and printed in a desktop publishing program. As one application, consider preparing an appendix for the test instruments used in a study. Rather than take photocopies of the test instructions, for example, these can be scanned and then formatted in a word processor. This helps to maintain a uniform appearance throughout a document and results in a more professional looking product.

Management and Presentation Tools

While certain software turns a personal computer into a text or publishing tool, other software can turn it into a management or presentation tool.

Spreadsheets

One of the earliest applications of personal computers which more than any other promoted the popularity of computers was the electronic spreadsheet. A spreadsheet has a multitude of uses but one that bears on assignment and thesis writing concerns certain aspects of project management. For example, an investigator may be tracking returns of questionnaires in a survey, student responses in an experiment, observations of weather conditions over time, or project costs. For any activity where a matrix of rows and columns is used for recording, the electronic spreadsheet can prove a versatile tool. It may serve in one instance to tabulate data; in another to generate totals, averages or trends; and in yet another for direct input into a statistical analysis program. Most users find that when they start to use spreadsheets, they soon discover numerous other ways these may be applied. The application is included here because many students find it valuable for managing different aspects of their research.

Statistical Analysis

Complex statistical analysis of data, once accessible only on large mainframe computers, now can be performed on personal computers. It is beyond the scope of this book to detail the kinds of parametric and nonparametric statistical analyses available in different programs, other than to note that with copy and paste functions it is relatively simple to import the results of any statistical testing directly into a word processing document. For those disciplines where field studies, surveys or experiments are typical, students may want to consider a statistical program that is compatible with a selected word processor in the sense of enabling easy transfer of results from one to the other.

Graphs and Charts

In the previous section on desktop publishing, mention is made of incorporating graphics and other art work in a printed assignment or thesis. In the days before computers, students either made drawings themselves or, more likely in the case of theses, had these professionally drawn. Today there are many programs for producing book quality diagrams on personal computers easily and quickly.

Real examples from university projects and theses illustrate some possibilities. Figure 5.4 shows a map of the distribution of all Wesleyan church buildings built before 1900 in the Adelaide area, but excluding inner Adelaide and North Adelaide townships. This schematic representation, drawn with a graphics program, shows the location of early churches along Adelaide's arterial roads.

A pie graph depicting the incidence of types of child abuse obtained in a survey of metropolitan schools is illustrated in Figure 5.5. The figure was produced in a graphing program and brought into a word processing document where an appropriate figure number and caption were added.

Figure 5.6 depicts an educational activity in mathematics. The drawings were scanned (see *Scanners*, page 51), imported into a graphics program and the text added. The figure then was placed in a word processing document that was a report of a project.

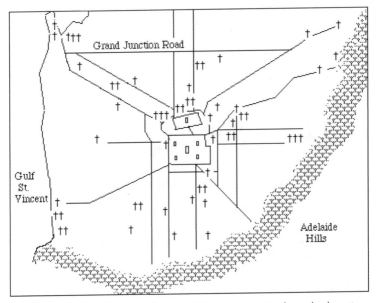

Figure 5.4 A map drawn with a graphics program to show the location of church buildings along Adelaide's arterial roads

The examples in Figures 5.4–5.6, from an Honours thesis, an essay and a term paper, demonstrate how graphic and paint tools may be applied and the resulting drawings added to any printed project. Most graphic tools allow drawings to be scaled proportionally and desktop publishing programs help to provide their precise placement on a page.

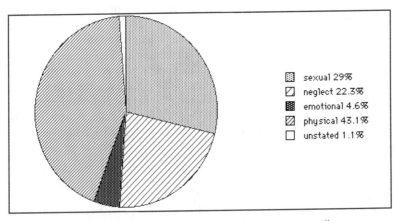

Figure 5.5 A pie graph drawn with a graphing program to illustrate survey data on incidence of child abuse

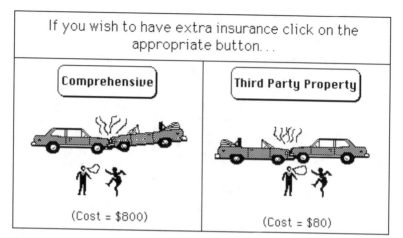

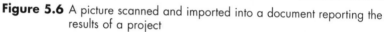

Figure 5.6 A picture scanned and imported into a document reporting the results of a project

Indexes and Tables of Contents

Two further electronic tools can prove useful in presenting the finished piece of writing. One compiles an index and the second prepares a table of contents or lists of tables and figures.

Compiling an Index

Most published textbooks have indexes that are designed to provide a quick means of locating particular topics. While few, if any, assignments or theses have indexes, an index facility in conjunction with a word processor can help in compiling lists of references. Electronic index programs usually work by users identifying index entries with a code (which is hidden so that it does not appear when the document is printed). The program then assembles all the coded entries, ignoring duplicates, and sorts them into an alphabetic listing of index entries with accompanying page numbers. To compile a bibliography of all authors cited, simply index each author and the program returns a complete alphabetic list of references to which publication details may be added. Gone is the worry of not including all sources referred to in a bibliography. The page numbers generated by the index feature will not be needed although these are useful for checking purposes.

Preparing a Table of Contents

A word processor facility for preparing a table of contents is a sure way that all headings and subheadings in the text, together with page numbers, correspond with those in the table of contents. The same facility may be used to compile a list of tables and a list of figures, again with the guarantee that captions of all tables and figures correspond with those listed in the contents pages.

An Invaluable Tool for Assignment and Thesis Writing

The computer is an *almost anything tool*. Change the software and the computer is transformed into a different tool. It is no exaggeration to say that the computer has had a dramatic impact on the way that assignments and theses are written and produced, just as it has impinged on so many other facets of daily life.

This chapter provides an overview of those software programs that can help in the many tasks involved in writing assignments and theses. From a knowledge of what programs are available in general terms and what different programs are designed to do, students can judge what tools are most helpful for the kinds of writing demanded in different fields. As with other aspects of scholarly writing, it is best to begin preparation early.

THE COMPUTER AS AN INFORMATION TOOL

Indispensable as the computer is as a writing and publishing tool for assignments or theses (described in Chapter 5), it is becoming equally indispensable as a tool for accessing information. This chapter describes the virtual library and its rich storehouse of electronic information resources.

Electronic Information Resources

Today's modern university and college library has undergone a wonderful transformation. Gone are the drawers of library cards recording details of all the library's holdings. In their place are computer workstations where students and researchers can rapidly check the availability of books and periodicals by author, title or call number. Where there are several libraries on campus, users can determine where a particular work is located, find out whether it is on the shelf or on loan, place a reservation on it if they wish, and later even renew the period of loan. Furthermore, users can often do all of this without even going to the library, by means of computers networked to the library's cataloguing system. And browsing through an electronic catalogue can often bring to light related works of high potential interest.

But the transformation of libraries goes far beyond the electronic cataloguing system. Also available from computer workstations in the library, or by remote access if you have a computer network connection to the library, are links to vast electronic information resources. Reference and subject librarians will happily show you what can be accessed from your particular library. This chapter provides just a taste of the rich information store available at your fingertips.

Online Literature Searches

Online literature searches of databases are called *online* since users connect to remote databases to access machine-readable information stored on large computers frequently located interstate or overseas using a personal computer, modem and telephone line. Online searching is a convenient means of gaining access to vast storehouses of information. The information is available virtually instantly and may be downloaded to the user's computer.

One major information provider is *Dialog* which has nearly 500 commercial databases covering a wide range of disciplines from agriculture through to zoology. Another is *Presscom*, a database of major Australian newspapers (excluding the Fairfax press). The *Australian Bibliographic Network* (ABN) is a further provider. Librarians at any university library can help access these and other databases. Since costs vary, according not only to the quality and type of information provided but to time spent online, librarians usually prefer to conduct online searches for users, based on descriptors furnished by those seeking information. Until a few years ago, online literature searches were the accepted way for all researchers to conduct systematic reviews of work in particular fields or topics.

Then a new medium emerged.

CD-ROM Databases

Termed 'the new papyrus', CD-ROM changed the way computers are used to store and retrieve information. Optical discs, similar to audio compact discs or CDs, hold staggering amounts of information that can be read by a personal computer. The information can only be read, not amended or added to, and hence the term *read only memories* or ROMs. Because of their vast storage capacity, CD-ROMs became the preferred medium for many information services. Libraries prefer them because there are no online telephone charges. For users, they are powerful research tools since the researcher interacts directly with the information base. On top of all of this, CD-ROMs can contain sound, pictures and animation in addition to text.

Rather than conduct online literature searches for others, librarians now conduct courses to show users how to access CD-ROM holdings themselves. So popular has this medium become that hundreds of CD-ROM titles are available for individual purchase. Users now can readily access electronic references like the *Oxford English Dictionary*. Another commercially available CD-ROM contains the complete unabridged text of nearly 2000 classic works (biographies, essays, dramatic works, letters, historical documents, poems, fictional works, tales of travel) together with pictures and narrations. The days of the printed encyclopedia are numbered as they are replaced by their electronic counterparts, published on silver-coated plastic disks using retrieval software that permits rapid searching. *Groliers Encyclopedia*, *Encarta* and *Encyclopedia Britannica* are all available in electronic form incorporating text, images, animation and sound. There is not space here other than to touch on a few electronic information resources.

Bookshelf is a CD-ROM containing a library of reference tools for writers, including resources such as the *American Heritage Dictionary*, *Roget's Electronic Thesaurus*, the *World Almanac and Book of Facts*, the *Columbia Dictionary of Quotations*, the *People's Chronology* and *Hammond World Atlas*.

SilverPlatter is one of the major new information providers for student and academic researchers with a large number of databases on compact disc. Included among these are the following:

Biological Abstracts — bibliographic citations and abstracts of current research in all the life sciences: biochemistry, biotechnology, ecology, immunology, microbiology, pharmacology, public health and toxicology.

CINAHL — the cumulative index to Nursing and Allied Health Literature covering all English language nursing journals and journals from allied health disciplines.

EconLit — citations and abstracts to journal articles, books, dissertations, conference proceedings in economics, econometrics, fiscal theory, public finance, management, law, demography, labour.

ERIC — bibliographic database consisting of Resources in Education (RIE) and the Current Index to Journals in Education (CIJE) covering the published journal literature from more than 775 periodicals.

MEDLINE — bibliographic citations and abstracts of biomedical literature in all languages drawn from the US National Library of Medicine from 1966 to the present.

PsycLit — an index of the world's serial literature in psychology and related disciplines of anthropology, education, linguistics, physiology, psychiatry and sociology, and drawn from articles in more than 1300 journals in thirty languages from fifty countries.

Sociofile — comprising Sociological Abstracts and Social Planning Policy and Development Abstracts, it contains indexes to and abstracts of the world's journal literature in sociology, and allied disciplines in social sciences dealing with culture and society.

CD-ROMs featuring Australian material include: *Supermap* which contains demographic data from the national census; *AUSTROM*, a collection of Australian databases produced by the National Library, with information on architecture, consumer services, criminology, education, family and society, language teaching for adults, library and information sciences, public affairs, tourism, sport and recreation; *The Parliament Stack* with information about Federal and State electorates, profiles of parliamentarians and past election results; and *Commonwealth Statutes* containing the full text of all acts in force since 1973, a list of repealed acts and a legislation index.

The 'new papyrus' is an apt description for the new storage medium of CD-ROM. More and more books, charts and photographs accumulated in libraries and museums are becoming available on convenient optical disc with accompanying software for rapid information searching and retrieving. CD-ROMs are as easy to access as computer disks and CD-ROM drives are now almost standard accessories in new computers.

Electronic Reference Library

Developments in library and information science are bringing about a fascinating evolution. The original online literature searches of remote databases via modem and telephone, which evolved to offline searches of CD-ROM databases, are now reverting to online searches of databases over wide area networks. Technology from SilverPlatter called Electronic Reference Library or ERL is making the virtual worldwide library a reality. ERL consists of software and protocols that many libraries, including most Australian university libraries, license in order to make available the most widely used databases that were previously available on CD-ROM over their campus networks.

What is claimed to be currently the most widely used search and retrieval software in the world, SPIRS (SilverPlatter Information Retrieval System), allows users on Macintosh, PCs or UNIX computers to access databases on an ERL server. Because data are stored on hard disk, searching and retrieving of information is five to ten times faster than on CD-ROM. A greater number of databases, and even a mixture of different databases, can be searched simultaneously.

Each university subscribing to Electronic Reference Library selects those databases that are most pertinent to the areas of study offered. Included at most university libraries are the AUSTROM collection of twelve Australian databases, Business Australia on Disc (a collection of eleven databases), Heritage and Environment (thirteen Australian databases) and a selection of the major SilverPlatter databases (EconLit, ERIC, MEDLINE, PsycLit, Sociofile).

The Internet and the World Wide Web

What started out as a military network in the United States, and then as a network for academic researchers in that country, has become a vast matrix of local, metropolitan, regional and national computer networks that span the globe. This complex of telephone wire, fibre optic cable and earth–satellite connections linking millions of computers around the world in hand-shaking agreements is commonly called the Internet or Net. Its growth in the 1990s has been staggering and no end to this dramatic growth is yet in sight.

What is particularly exciting about the Internet is not so much the inter-connection of computers across the globe but rather the information that resides on all of these computers. The linking of computer networks across countries makes available an enormous information resource, the World Wide Web, that may be described as the world's largest library. Via the World Wide Web, or *Web* as it is increasingly called, a rapidly accumu-lating store of information can be accessed that was previously located in millions of separate titles in individual libraries throughout the world. The Web also contains a rich store of up-to-the-minute information from news and other media sources. Often the Web leads other mass media with news-breaking events. Furthermore, this immense storehouse of infor-mation is now available anywhere, anytime, to those with the appropriate tools — that is, the hardware, the software and the know-how.

The growth of the Web is being spurred on by the development of easy-to-use browser software tools like Netscape Navigator and Microsoft Internet Explorer that utilise hypertext, the electronic nodes or hyperlinks that connect one piece of text or image with another. By clicking on hyper-text links in Web pages, usually indicated in colour on colour monitors or underlined on black and white monitors, readers can branch elsewhere on the same Web page, branch to another Web page on the same computer, or indeed to any Web page anywhere on the Internet. The world information store becomes an open book.

With the Internet and the World Wide Web, researchers, students and individuals in the community now have at their fingertips the resources of a worldwide storehouse of information, vastly more comprehensive than that contained in any single library or museum, and in many ways easier to locate. All this information may be viewed or downloaded to a computer at university or home. Through the Web, or with specialist software, users may also send messages electronically (email) to colleagues or fellow students almost anywhere in the world. Distance ceases to be a barrier.

Cautions with Web Materials

What is the downside of what seems like the utopian development of the Internet and the World Wide Web? First, the Web contains an immense amount of trivia, much information is transient, and some is biased or inaccurate. To this others might add that much is offensive, obscene and positively dangerous information. Of course, the print media are not always free from similar criticisms, but printed sources usually undergo more stringent refereeing processes than currently does most information appearing on the Web. On the Web many can become publishers. What becomes crucially important then for researchers and students is to evaluate critically *all* information, whether this comes from electronic or non-electronic data sources.

A second difficulty about online information sources like Web pages is how to cite these in assignments and theses. Because the Internet and the Web are relatively new, procedures for referencing online sources are still evolving. Guidelines for referencing Web and other electronic sources, together with traditional printed sources, are found in Chapter 13.

A third potential danger about Web materials, associated with referencing, is the critical need to acknowledge sources. The situation is no different from the need to acknowledge sources in journals and books, but with the ease of downloading material from the Internet and the facility of word processors to copy and paste, it becomes even more important to note all words that are not your own and to record the source of all quotations. See the section on Taking Notes in Chapter 2 and heed carefully the cautions there about plagiarism. The facility of word and text processors to find words or phrases in electronic materials makes it in some ways easier to detect instances of suspected plagiarism.

Yet a further problem, or frustration, is that at times the Internet is slow (it has its peak traffic times too); at times it seems unreliable in that a hypertext link that you want to follow shows an error message (Web addresses do change and if you enter an address it must be entered exactly and without any spaces); and at times servers or the computers holding the information you want to see are not operational (possibly because of maintenance or perhaps because the site is too busy to handle another request at that moment). It is useful to know about these problems and to take into account that the Internet is still very much evolving.

Finding Your Way Around the Web

Like finding your way around the university library, finding your way around the Web requires you to know the locations or addresses of Web pages. Corresponding to the call number of books and journals, all Web pages have a uniform resource locator, or URL, that allows your network browser to locate them easily. To jump to a particular Web page, enter the desired URL in your browser, for example, type *http://www.flinders.edu.au* to go to the Flinders University of South Australia. From the Flinders

Home Page, as the first page of a Web site is called, point to any hypertext link and browse among the various faculties and the university library to find what is on offer.

To go back to a previous page, press the Back button on the Toolbar if you are using Netscape as browser to return to the page you looked at last. To return to a page you were at some steps before, you can usually view the history of where you have been browsing and, by pointing to a desired location, jump back there. You can also bookmark sites, recording in your browser those Web addresses to which you may wish to return. Hypertext links make it easy to traverse the Web, jumping from one Web site to another somewhere else in the world. Should you feel lost in cyberspace, the Home button on the Toolbar returns you to where you were at the start of a given session. Similar strategies on Microsoft Internet Explorer help you to find your way around the Web.

It is often useful to know where a Web page comes from, as this can sometimes aid in evaluating its content. Deciphering the components that comprise a URL helps here since every page on the Web has a URL or address on the Internet by which it is uniquely identified. Take the Big Read Bookstore, for example, whose URL (http://www.bigread.com.au) comprises components generally included in each URL:

- http:// indicates the Internet protocol for transferring information (it stands for hypertext transfer protocol)
- www indicates a server on the World Wide Web (that is, a computer connected to the Internet containing information for distribution)
- next comes the server name (e.g. Bigread, ANU, Qantas) of the company or institution
- this is followed by the type of organisation, for example:
  com — commercial
  edu — education
  gov — government
  mil — military
  net — network resources
  org — organisation
- finally, there is a two-digit country code, for example:
  au — Australia
  id — Indonesia
  nz — New Zealand
  sg — Singapore
  uk — United Kingdom.

(No country code is used for the US since the Internet originated there.) Thus, http://www.bigread.com.au tells us that this is a commercial Web site in Australia run by a company called bigread, in this case, the Big Read Bookstore.

Searching the Web

So much information is available on the Web that even if it were a static source (and it is not, it changes and grows constantly) it would take a lifetime to visit every page. How do you find specific information then when your assignment or thesis has strictly imposed deadlines? Fortunately, there are search engines to help. Search engines, as their name implies, are rather like machines (they are really computer programs) that trawl the Net in response to specific requests for information. Already there are many competing search engines from which to choose, and new and what are claimed to be better ones come on stream from time to time. Among the better known search engines are Lycos, WebCrawler, Yahoo!, Hotbot, Excite and AltaVista.

Using what are variously called robots, crawlers, spiders or scooters, the different search engines roam the Internet compiling indexes of URLs or Web addresses. Some search engines operate by organising information into categories. Yahoo!, for instance, has categories for Arts and Humanities, Computers and Internet, Education, News and Media, Science (to list a few), and within each of these categories are further sub-categories that lead in turn to yet further sub-categories, rather like a tree with progressive layers of roots. Searching with Yahoo! is an easy and quick way to begin an information search and progressively narrow the search to a smaller number of related areas. You may still be surprised to find several hundred or even several thousand sites that match your particular field of interest.

Other search engines, such as AltaVista, operate by seeking to compile an index of the occurrence of every word of every Web page on the Net. The magnitude of the task is breathtaking: scooters working around the clock search for new Web pages and return to base where each word in a document and its associated URL is added to a growing, dynamic database. Knowing how such engines work demonstrates the necessity to be as specific as possible with requests for information. A search for 'Internet', for example, will result in a list of not only several thousand but several million Web sites that match the query. However, if you add further words or phrases to your search query, combining these with Boolean operators (AND, OR and NOT), you can frequently find information that fairly precisely matches what you are looking for. Examples best illustrate successful strategies to narrow a search. While these examples apply to a particular search engine, the use of Boolean operators and somewhat similar strategies hold for others.

Simple Searches

When you search with AltaVista, you may choose between what is called *Simple Search* and *Advanced Search*. A few examples, as given in Table 6.1, best illustrate some Simple Search techniques.

Table 6.1 Simple searches of the Internet with AltaVista

Enter the word(s) below in the Search field	to find Web pages containing occurrences of
1 reading	the word *reading*
2 reading comprehension	the word *reading* or the word *comprehension*
3 reading +comprehension	the word *reading* and the word *comprehension*
4 reading −university	excludes from (1) pages containing, for example, *Reading University*
5 "reading comprehension"	the phrase *reading comprehension*
6 comprehen*	the words *comprehend, comprehends, comprehending, comprehension,* . . .
7 reading +comprehen* −university	the word *reading* (but excluding *Reading University*) and the words *comprehend, comprehends, comprehending, comprehension,* . . .

Simple searches with AltaVista can be quite elaborate as the examples in Table 6.1 illustrate, and often these suffice for many information searches. However, more versatile still is AltaVista's Advanced Search engine.

Advanced Searches

Advanced Searches with AltaVista are characterised by the use of the Boolean operators AND, OR and NOT (in place of + and − in Simple Search) and the operator NEAR. Again, examples best illustrate some of the possibilities with Advanced Search (see Table 6.2).

The searches in Table 6.2 are a small sample of what is possible but these illustrate the power and versatility of AltaVista. With Advanced Search, you may also order the results of a search query in terms of which are placed first, and you can further limit searches by specifying dates.

Table 6.2 Advanced searches of the Internet with AltaVista

Enter the word(s) below in the Search field	to find Web pages containing occurrences of
1 hypertext OR literacy	the word *hypertext* or the word *literacy*
2 hypertext AND literacy	the words *hypertext* and *literacy* (this is a more restricted search than OR above)
3 "Myers-Briggs personality scale"	the phrase *Myers-Briggs personality scale*
4 "basic skills" AND assessment	the phrase *basic skills* and the word *assessment*
5 John NEAR Kennedy	*John Kennedy, John F. Kennedy, John and the Kennedy brothers* (and all other phrases where John and Kennedy occur within 10 words of each other)
6 "computer anxiety" AND (assessment OR measure*)	the phrase *computer anxiety* together with either the word *assessment* or any of *measure, measures, measurement* . . .
7 readability AND (graphic* OR picture* OR image* OR illustration*)	the word *readability* together with any of *graphic/s, picture/s image/s* or *illustration/s*

Learning on the Net

In its role as an information tool, the Web is widely used to present information about the Internet itself and about Internet tools and protocols. Macquarie University Library, for instance, has developed a self-instruction program for students (and staff) that is delivered on the Web. Called *World Wide Web Walkabout*, the training program provides instruction on Web tools like electronic mail (email), newsgroups, listservs, telnet and FTP. At a second level the program provides practice in the use of Web tools through particular disciplinary areas (Sociology, American Politics, Fine Arts, and so on).

With the realisation that the Web is a powerful information tool, more and more universities and TAFE colleges are offering selected courses online, if not as a replacement then as a supplementary mode of delivery.

Online Databases

Because of the popularity of the Internet and its ease of use, many commercial information providers are making materials available (for a fee) to online searching. Again the reference or subject librarians are the most useful points of contact about which materials are available at your library.

One such online database is FirstSearch which includes a number of periodical indexes and databases of abstracts. Table 6.3 lists a few of the many FirstSearch databases that students might find most useful. In addition, FirstSearch contains databases in arts and humanities, business and economics, education, engineering and technology, life sciences, medicine and the health sciences, public affairs and law, and the social sciences.

Table 6.3 A selection of FirstSearch databases available on the Internet

Name of database	Description of contents
Article1st	Index of articles from more than 12 000 journals
Contents1st	Table of contents from more than 12 000 journals
Papers1st	Index of papers presented at conferences
Proceedings1st	Index of conference publications
Diss	Dissertation Abstracts
MicrocomputerAbs	Microcomputer Abstracts
NewsAbs	Abstracts of newspaper articles from more than 25 newspapers

Other highly useful online databases include *Current Contents* which indexes the contents of approximately 7000 journals in arts and humanities, science, and social sciences; and *Lexis-Nexis*, a fully searchable database containing the complete text of many newspapers around the world and a large number of journals across a range of disciplines.

Indispensable Research Tool

Computer software developers are fond of describing their products as transparent or seamless by which they mean that individuals can use programs or operating systems naturally and with minimum instruction. Certainly the rapid expansion of the Internet and its widespread acceptance is due to the seamless way that Network browsers such as Netscape enable users to navigate the World Wide Web without the need for arcane instructions or detailed knowledge of computer protocols. Similarly, literature searching, once the preserve of highly trained librarians, is a skill that students can, with help, develop themselves. Again, software has made the search of electronic resources, whether in remote databases or on CD-ROMs stored on local servers, seamless to users.

No longer are students and researchers bound by their locally based libraries. With appropriate technology such as Electronic Reference Library and access to the Internet, students completing assignments and theses can search for and retrieve electronic information across institutions and across worldwide networks. The computer becomes an indispensable research tool.

Part II

WRITING THE ASSIGNMENT OR THESIS

 **C** h a p t e r

COMMON FEATURES OF EDITORIAL STYLE

Every writing genre has a particular style that sets it apart from other genres. So it is with assignment and thesis writing. The editorial style for writing at the tertiary level includes the various rules and conventions that are accepted for scholarly writing. Some of these such as the avoidance of personal reference, colloquialisms, jargon, sexist language, stereotyping and ethnic bias, apply to writing style and are addressed in Chapter 1. This chapter focuses more on editorial style as it applies particularly to assignment and thesis writing. Rules for capitalisation, the use of italics, conventions for numbers, and shortened forms are noted briefly. Observance of editorial conventions helps to ensure consistency in presentation, thus freeing readers to focus properly on writing content.

Capitalisation

Titles of Books, Journals and Other Works

The practice recommended in this book is to use capitals for the initial letters of key words in titles of books and journal titles (that is, capitalise all words other than prepositions, conjunctions and articles). This convention, termed *title case*, applies to citations in the text and to references in bibliographies:

History of Australia since the Second World War

A similar practice applies to titles of plays, films, musical compositions, works of art, newspapers and magazines, as well as to published and unpublished test instruments.

Journal Articles

For journal articles and theses, capitals are used for the first letter of the first word and of the first word following a colon, and for proper nouns. This convention is termed *sentence case*:

> New technologies: Effective tools for Australian classrooms

Proper Nouns and Adjectives

The initial letter of proper nouns and adjectives is capitalised. Two exceptions are roman when reference is to *roman type* or *roman numerals*, and *arabic* when referring to *arabic numerals*.

Initial capitals are not used for teaching departments or universities (as in this sentence) unless reference is made to a specific department or university:

> The Department of Anatomy at Sydney University

Botanical and zoological names are capitalised when referring to order, family and genus. The name of a species, however, consists of two words of which only the first (the name of the genus) has a capital:

> The blue gum belongs to the myrtle family, Myrtaceae, in the genus *Eucalyptus*; its species is *Eucalyptus globulus*.

Nouns Followed by Numerals or Letters

Use capitals for references to specific tables, figures, experiments, trials, chapters:

> Table 12, Figure 3, Experiment 2, Trial 3, Chapter 4

but not for elements of tables or books such as rows, columns or pages:

> row 2, column 3, page 4, pages 21-24

When reference is to *this chapter* or *the next chapter*, there is no capital.

Headings and Subheadings

Chapter 9 deals with levels of headings within assignments or theses, and recommends use of upper and lower case to distinguish between levels of headings. At the top level (e.g. for chapter titles) full capitalisation is common; at the next level down, title case is usual; while at the bottom level, sentence case is the norm. Practice depends on the number of levels of headings. See Chapter 9 for details.

Table and Figure Captions

Captions for tables and figures commonly use sentence case. The same practice applies to table headings and to legends for figures.

Italics

Titles

Italics are used in references or text when reference is made to titles of published works: books, journals, plays, films, musical compositions, newspapers and magazines, as well as to paintings and sculpture.

Cited Letters, Words or Phrases

When a letter, word or phrase is cited in the text as an example, such examples are commonly italicised. Quotation marks may sometimes be used instead. Word processors and printers, however, are making the use of italics more common:

> The term *title case* refers to the use of initial capitals in key words in titles of books and journals.

> Australian spelling favours the use of *s* rather than *z* in words like *italicise*, *capitalise*, *standardise*, and so on.

Italics are also used for letters referring to statistical tests, and in algebraic expressions:

> The t and F tests were used...

> $b(x) + a \sin x$

Typesetting convention does not italicise mathematical functions such as log, sine and cosine.

Foreign Words and Abbreviations

Foreign words are commonly placed in italics. So many foreign words have come into the English language, however, that foreign words are not always easily recognisable. The Australian *Style Manual* recommends that, if words are included in the *Macquarie Dictionary*, where roman type is used for all words irrespective of origin, then such words are considered anglicised. Therefore, if a foreign word or phrase is not included in the *Macquarie*, it should probably be italicised:

> *Gracias*

Most Latin abbreviations now are regarded as sufficiently common as not to require the use of italics, though the longer form of any such abbreviation is italicised as a foreign word:

e.g. abbreviation for *exempli gratia*, for example

et al. abbreviation for *et alii*, and others

Table B.1, included in Appendix B, lists abbreviations commonly used in assignments and theses together with meanings and examples.

Scientific Names

Scientific names of animals and plants, from the taxonomic level of genus downwards, are italicised. Some generic names, however, have come into common usage, in which case italics are not used (e.g. eucalyptus):

Kangaroo rats belong to the family Heteromyidae in the genus *Dipodomys*.

Eucalyptus trees belong to the myrtle family, Myrtaceae, in the genus *Eucalyptus*.

Numbers

The convention on the use of numbers recommended in this book is to spell out all one-digit numbers and to use figures for numbers containing two or more digits. This convention is becoming more widespread than the one stating that numbers less than one hundred be spelled out, especially in papers containing many numbers. However, there are several exceptions to whichever rule is followed.

Numbers that Begin a Sentence

A number beginning a sentence is spelled out regardless of its size:

One hundred and twenty-eight students were included in the survey.

Note the hyphenation in numbers when spelled out such as *twenty-eight*, *thirty-two*, *sixty-seven* and so on.

Quoting Percentages

Figures are used in quoting percentages.

The class roll showed that 9 per cent of children were absent.

Note that *per* and *cent* are two words, but *percentage* and *percentile* are single words.

Street Numbers, Dates and Times

Street numbers, dates and time of day (when used with a.m. or p.m.) are always expressed in figures.

> He moved into 10 Downing Street.
>
> The election was held on October 6.
>
> Testing commenced at 10.30 a.m.

Numbers in Tables

Table numbers and reference to numbers in tables are never spelled out:

> Reference to Table 2 shows that the Central district received 18 centimetres of rain in February and the Northern district, 9 centimetres.

Fractions and Ordinal Numbers

Fractions are usually spelled out unless part of a large number:

> The families spent one fifth of their income on accommodation.

Rules for ordinal numbers (first, second, third ... 10th ...) follow the same rules as indicated for cardinal numbers (one, two, three ... 10 ...) above:

> The students were in the fourth grade.
>
> The second item of the 16th trial.

Series of Numbers

Where there is a series of numbers, some of which have one digit and some more than one digit, the numbers are expressed in figures:

> The subject scored 9, 11, 8, 13 and 12 over five trials.

Plurals of Numbers

The plural of dates and numbers is formed by adding *s* or *es*:

> 1980s
>
> three fours and two sixes

Shortened Forms

Abbreviations and Full Stops

The general rule is to use a full stop if an abbreviation does not end with the letter of the word being abbreviated:

p.   pp.   Vic.   Jan.   ibid.   loc.cit.

but to omit periods if the abbreviation and word end with the same letter:

Qld   vols   Dept

Using Shortened Forms

Generally, shortened forms should be defined *before* use; once defined, the shortened form may be used:

The Australian Reading Association (ARA) was formed in 1975. ARA now has a membership of ...

If the shortened form is so well known as not to cause confusion, definition is unnecessary:

Qantas   Unesco   USSR   ACTU

The abbreviation *etc.* (*et cetera*) is often a sign of lazy writing. Its use is to be discouraged.

Similarly, the use of the ampersand character (&), in place of *and*, is such a small saving of space that its use is not recommended here. In disciplines like Psychology, however, ampersand is used in references for joint authorship (e.g. Walker & Hess).

The shortened forms mostly derived from Latin (such as e.g. i.e. ibid. loc.cit.), a full list of which is given in Table B.1 (Appendix B), are generally reserved for use in footnotes and references. In the body of the text such abbreviations should occur only in parentheses or in tables or figures, and are not italicised.

Special Symbols

Shortened forms are often used, especially in tables or figures, though such use needs generally to be defined either in the caption or in a footnote. This ruling applies to all but the most common abbreviations encountered in mathematical and scientific writing such as:

cm	centimetre(s)	p	probability
km	kilometre(s)	F	Fahrenheit or F-ratio
sin	sine	log	logarithm

Special symbols similarly may be used in tables and figures to save space, but again these should be defined in a caption, footnote or legend. However, many symbols encountered in mathematical and scientific writing such as the following are so common as not to require definition:

$$< \quad > \quad \Sigma \quad \Pi \quad \circ \quad ' \quad '' \quad \mu \quad \sigma$$

A good rule to follow with all shortened forms is *spell out if there is any doubt*.

Other General Features

The following additional points regarding format can aid readability and the general appearance of printed text:

1. Only one space is necessary after a full stop and other punctuation marks. The practice of two spaces was a convention adopted in typewritten papers. This practice is no longer recommended, especially for fully justified text since it often leads to *rivers of white*.
2. Underlining now is generally replaced by the use of italics or boldface in papers produced with a word processor. The practice of underlining is another relic of the days of typewriters.
3. Paragraphs may be indented or additional spacing left between paragraphs. To do both is unnecessary. Following a heading, it is common practice not to indent the first paragraph.
4. The first sentence following a heading should stand alone and not depend on the heading to complete its meaning.
5. Take care with sentences containing an unaccompanied *this*. Nearly always there is reference to something preceding. Repetition of the noun or the use of a synonym can enhance comprehension.

Fonts and Point Sizes

Now that a majority of assignments and theses are written on computers, some consideration needs to be given to type of font (sometimes referred to as *typeface* which, strictly speaking, is the correct typesetting term) and point size.

The first choice is whether to use a serif or sans serif font. Serifs are the small strokes at the ends of letters, used originally by stonemasons to finish off a main stroke such as a capital T. Sans serif means literally *without serifs*. Table 7.1 illustrates four commonly used fonts, two serif fonts and two sans serif fonts.

There is some evidence that serifs help guide the eye from one word to the next, enhancing legibility and, accordingly, serif fonts are normally used in books and magazines for the main text. Their use is recommended also in assignments and theses. Sans serif fonts are commonly applied to headings in magazines.

Table 7.1 Samples of serif and sans serif fonts

Common serif fonts	Common sans serif fonts
This text is in Palatino. This text is in Times.	This text is in Geneva. This text is in Helvetica.

The four fonts illustrated in Table 7.1 are proportionally spaced, the letter *i*, for example, taking less space than *m*. In a monospaced font, by contrast, each letter occupies the same width. Courier is an example of a monospaced font.

```
This is text in 12-point Courier to
simulate a typewriter.
```

Size of font is measured in points. However, the proportions of the letters vary in different fonts, producing a marked difference in apparent size, as Table 7.2 illustrates. See also Table 7.1, where all the examples are in 12-point type.

Table 7.2 Point size in two commonly used fonts (Palatino and Times)

10-point Palatino	This is a sample of text in 10-point Palatino.
12-point Palatino	This is a sample of text in 12-point Palatino.
14-point Palatino	This is a sample of text in 14-point Palatino.
10-point Times	This is a sample of text in 10-point Times.
12-point Times	This is a sample of text in 12-point Times.
14-point Times	This is a sample of text in 14-point Times.

The choice of which font and what point size is determined, first, by what is available for whatever word processor and printer are being used and, second, by personal preference. Commonly used point sizes and fonts for the main text (and headings) in assignments and theses are 12-point Palatino or 14-point Times. Slightly more compact is 10-point Palatino or 12-point Times. Smaller point sizes are commonly used in tables while other fonts may be used for special symbols or in figures.

Usage and Editorial Style

This chapter does no more than touch on certain problem areas relating to usage and editorial style in assignment and thesis writing. Students are encouraged to follow up as necessary the much more detailed treatment given in the Australian *Style Manual for Authors, Printers and Editors* and other style manuals listed in Appendix A. Chapters 8 to 14 focus more specifically on editorial conventions relating to quoting and referencing, and the layout of pages, tables, figures and appendixes.

Not all authorities agree on matters of editorial style, and editorial styles, like fashions, do change. Students need to find out what conventions apply in particular fields and, above all, be consistent in their usage. The conventions described in this chapter and followed in this book are applicable to a wide cross-section of disciplines.

**C** h a p t e r

THE GENERAL
FORMAT

In presenting an assignment or thesis, there are a number of format specifications that the writer should follow. These specifications are not to stifle writers but rather to allow them to encompass their individual contributions within a conventional framework that is both logical and sequential. By following stringent format requirements, writers not only can systematise and structure their thinking in terms of theme, unity and clarity, but they also can facilitate the reading and interpretation of the work by others.

By convention, a paper (using this term to refer to term assignments, theses and research reports) consists of three parts: the preliminaries, the text and the reference materials. The length of any of these three parts is conditional on the extent of the study. In a long paper, each of the main parts may consist of several subsections; in a short paper, materials preceding the text might include only a title page while the reference material might be limited to a listing of basic references.

The order in which individual items within the three main sections commonly appear is outlined below, although not every paper includes all the items listed. Frequently, certain departments or faculties have special specifications that diverge from this conventional pattern, but the following sequence is generally accepted:

1. *The Preliminaries*
   (a) Title page and Abstract
   (b) Declaration
   (c) Acknowledgments

(d) Table of contents

(e) List of tables

(f) List of figures or illustrations

2. *The Text*

(a) Introduction (introductory chapter or chapters)

(b) Main body of the report (usually divided into chapters and sections)

(c) Conclusion (summary chapter or chapters)

3. *The Reference Material*

(a) References

(b) Appendix (or Appendixes)

The order of (a) and (b) may be reversed.

(c) Index (if any)

The Preliminaries

Title Page

Most universities prescribe their own form of title page for theses, dissertations and research papers, and these should be complied with in all matters of content and spacing. Generally, the following information is required:

Written Assignment

- Title of the assignment
- Name of the writer
- Name of the course and lecturer for whom the assignment is written
- Name of the department
- Name of the university, college or institution
- Date on which the paper is due and, sometimes, the date when submitted.

Thesis

- Title of the thesis
- Designation of faculty (optional)
- Name of the institution to which the thesis is being submitted
- Degree for which the thesis is presented
- Name of the candidate (if desired, degrees may be listed after the name)
- Month and year of submission of thesis

Figures 8.1 and 8.2 illustrate typical title pages for an assignment and a thesis respectively.

A CRITICAL EXAMINATION OF THE ROLE OF
TRADE UNIONS IN AUSTRALIA 1890–1990

by

K. Beattie

Modern History 1A — Lecturer: P. Smith

Department of History

University of Western Australia

23rd October, 1996

Figure 8.1 Sample title page for a written assignment

A GEOLOGICAL SURVEY OF SOIL EROSION

ALONG THE NEW SOUTH WALES COASTLINE

by

Matthew Hamilton-Smith, B.Sc. (Hons.)

A dissertation submitted in partial
fulfilment of the requirements for
the degree of Doctor of Philosophy
in the University of Sydney

February, 1997

Figure 8.2 Sample title page of a thesis

Subject to the special requirements of individual institutions, the best practice is to centre the title of the paper on the page in upper case letters. Where the title is too long to be centred on one line, line breaks should be made at convenient points to avoid splitting phrases. Titles may be in bold-face but not usually underlined or placed within inverted commas. Below the title, material may be centred or balanced against the left and right margins of the page.

Abstract

In some departments and institutions an abstract may be required. An abstract consists of the following parts:
- a short statement of the problem
- a brief description of the methods and procedures adopted
- a condensed summary of the findings of the study.

The length of the abstract may be specified — for example, 200 words. Usually an abstract is short. In some cases the abstract is bound into the thesis; in others, it is printed on a separate sheet and placed inside the front cover. If included in the thesis, it is placed immediately following the title page. For an assignment, the abstract is often placed on the same page as the title. For both theses and assignments, the abstract is normally preceded by a centred capitalised heading ABSTRACT, and the first paragraph is not indented.

Declaration

For theses it is usual to include a short statement declaring that the thesis has not previously been submitted for any degree, and that acknowledgments have been made to the contributions of others where appropriate. The statement is usually a single paragraph, not indented, and under a centred heading DECLARATION, usually in capitals. The statement is signed by the author of the thesis. Institutions often specify the precise form of wording to be used such as that in Figure 8.3.

DECLARATION

I certify that this thesis does not incorporate without acknowledgment any material previously submitted for a degree or diploma in any university; and that to the best of my knowledge and belief it does not contain any material previously published or written by another person where due reference is not made in the text.

Figure 8.3 Sample wording for declaration for a thesis

Acknowledgments

Acknowledgments recognise the persons to whom the writer is indebted for guidance and assistance during the study, and credit institutions for providing funds to implement the study or for use of personnel, facilities and other resources. For a term paper or written assignment, it is not necessary to acknowledge staff or institutions. If the list of acknowledgments is short, the heading *Acknowledgments* is omitted and a brief statement containing the acknowledgments is placed slightly above the centre of the page. Such a practice would be necessary for the brief acknowledgment in Figure 8.4.

> Thanks are due to the Department of School Health Services, the Queensland Radium Institute, the Institute of Child Guidance, the Medical School, the University of Queensland, and members of the Australian Medical Association for their interest, assistance and support in the preparation of this report.

Figure 8.4 Brief acknowledgment for a term report

To obtain a clear idea of what is included in lists of acknowledgments within separate departments, writers are advised to examine a number of written reports and theses to determine the approach usually taken within their own discipline. In all instances, scholarly honesty demands that assistance be acknowledged, always within the confines of simplicity and tact.

Table of Contents

The table of contents includes the major divisions of the thesis: the introduction, the chapters with their subsections, and the references and appendix. Page numbers for each of these divisions are given. Care should be taken that titles of chapters and captions of subdivisions within chapters correspond exactly with those included in the body of the report. In some cases, subheadings within chapters are not included in the table of contents, although this is mandatory for many institutions. It is optional whether acknowledgments, list of tables and list of figures are placed in the table of contents. The purpose of a table of contents is to provide an analytical overview of the material included in the study or report together with the sequence of presentation. To this end, the relationship between major divisions and minor subdivisions needs to be shown by an appropriate use of capitalisation and indentation or by using a numeric system.

The setting out of a sample table of contents is shown in Figure 8.5. The heading TABLE OF CONTENTS, typically in capitals, is centred at the top of the page. Below this appears the heading *Page* at the right margin. Then come abstract, declaration, acknowledgments, list of tables and list of figures (if included). Below this again the heading *Chapter* appears at the left margin. Chapter titles, in full capitals or boldface, are typed without terminal punctuation and numbered consecutively in arabic numerals. Chapter headings normally are aligned under the chapter title, the initial letter of the first word and of all key words being capitalised. Subdivisions are indented and are similarly capitalised.

The preliminary pages are numbered using roman numerals (i, ii, iii ...). Note that the title page does not appear in the Table of Contents, though a page is assigned to it. Similarly, the Table of Contents itself has a page number assigned following the Acknowledgments. The body of the thesis and the reference material are numbered using arabic numerals (1, 2, 3 ...). Figure 8.5 illustrates these features.

A final table of contents cannot be prepared until the entire draft of a report or thesis is typed. Only then can page numbers be inserted. However, as each chapter or section is being written, it is helpful to develop a table of contents as a guide to the structure of the argument or thesis.

TABLE OF CONTENTS

(continued)

---

v

Figure 8.5 Sample table of contents for a thesis

An alternative method of presenting a table of contents works not only on a consistent principle of indentation, but also on the use of a numbering system. Figure 8.6 shows, for example, how Chapter 3 of the sample table of contents in Figure 8.5 could be set out using the full numbering system.

Figure 8.6 Alternative numbering system for headings and subheadings in table of contents

A table of contents is necessary only in those papers where the text has been divided into chapters or several subheadings. Most short written assignments do not require a table of contents. The basic criterion for the inclusion of subheadings under major chapter divisions is whether the procedure facilitates the reading of a report and especially the location of specific sections within a report.

List of Tables

Following the table of contents, the writer needs to prepare a list of tables. The heading, LIST OF TABLES, is usually centred in capitals on a separate page. Below this the headings *Table* and *Page* appear at the left and right margins respectively. For each table there is needed the table number in arabic numerals, the exact caption or title of the table and the page number. The initial letters of key words in titles are capitalised. No terminal punctuation is used. An example of the application of these format conventions is presented in Figure 8.7.

```
                    LIST OF TABLES
    Table                                          Page

    1  Total Population Distribution of
       Australia and its South East Asian
       Markets (in Thousands)                        26

    2  Percentage of Working Population Employed
       in Agriculture, Forestry and Fishing          54

    3  Percentage of Working Population
       Employed in Mining and Manufacturing          63

    4  Gross National Product per Head               71
```

Figure 8.7 Sample list of tables

List of Figures (or Illustrations)

The list of figures appears in the same form as the list of tables. The page is headed LIST OF FIGURES, without terminal punctuation, and the numbers of the figures are listed at the left of the page under the heading *Figure*. Normally arabic numerals are used for numbering. Page numbers appear under the heading *Page* at the right margin. If there are several illustrations of any one kind, for instance 10 or more maps in addition to other illustrations, a separate division and listing is necessary. For example, if there were 15 figures, 2 maps, and 4 photographs, there would be two separate divisions: LIST OF FIGURES (for the 15 figures) and LIST OF ILLUSTRATIONS (for the 2 maps and 4 photographs). The term *Plates* is often used for photographs. Plates are formatted similarly to figures. Examples are given in Figures 8.8, 8.9 and 8.10.

```
                    LIST OF FIGURES
    Figure                                         Page

    1  The Export-Import Cycle                       10

    2  Export-Import Index: Base 1990/91             21

    3  A Model for Analysing the Export-Import
       Process                                       26
```

Figure 8.8 Sample list of figures

```
LIST OF ILLUSTRATIONS
Figure                                              Page

1  Map of the New England Tableland
   in 1839                                          12

2  Diagrammatic Representation of First
   Land Trails                                      18

3  Subdivision of Early Settlement Areas            35
```

Figure 8.9 Sample list of illustrations

```
LIST OF PLATES
Plate                                               Page

1  HyperStory Title Card                            42

2  The Index Card Linked to All Cards               42

3  Page 1: Transparent Buttons Placed Over
   Many of the Words in Story                       44

4  Page 2: Picture Clues Scripted to Appear
   and then Disappear                               45

5  Page 3: A Card Picture with Digitised
   Speech Clues                                     47

6  Page 4: Text Made into a Cloze Exercise
   by Covering Words with Opaque Buttons            48
```

Figure 8.10 Sample list of plates

The Text

The main body of the thesis follows the preliminaries detailed above, and begins with the first page of the text. The text is the most important part of a thesis, as it is in this section that writers present the basic tenets of their arguments. Writers should devote most of their energies to a careful organisation and presentation of the findings or general argument. The more logically, concisely and coherently the writer develops the thesis through chapter divisions, the more readily the overall purpose and strength of a study become evident; and so the possibility is increased of convincing readers of the importance or power of an argument, or of a series of findings.

Short assignments do not necessarily have chapter divisions or subject headings, but there should be the same logical framework that is adopted for major theses: an introductory section or sections; the major report of the study, subdivided where appropriate; and a summary that contains the findings, conclusions and recommendations arising from the study. The organisation of the text needs careful planning so that each section or sub-division represents an important logical division of the topic being investigated and reported.

Introduction

An introduction should be written with considerable care, with two major aims in view: to introduce the problem in a suitable context, and to arouse and stimulate the reader's interest. If introductions are dull, aimless, confused and rambling, and lacking in precision, direction and specificity, there is little incentive for the reader to continue reading. The reader begins to expect an overall dullness and aimlessness in the whole paper. The length of an introduction varies according to the nature of the research project. For shorter written assignments (2000–3000 words), a single carefully structured introductory paragraph may suffice; for longer papers and theses, an introduction may be chapter length. An introductory chapter usually contains:

(a) a lucid, complete, and concise statement of the problem being investigated or the general purpose of the study

(b) a justification for the study, establishing the importance of the problem (In some disciplines, it is appropriate at this juncture to indicate the limitations of the project and to define terms used in the study that have a special meaning or significance for the investigation.)

(c) a preview of the organisation of the rest of the paper or thesis to assist readers in grasping the relationship between the various components

(d) in many disciplines, a resumé of the history and present status of the problem, delineated by a concise, critical review of previous studies into closely related problems (If this approach is adopted, it is important to discuss the contribution of these previous studies to the question being investigated, and to show how the present investigation either arises from contradictions or inadequacies of earlier investigations or builds on their findings.)

(e) a brief statement of the sources of data, the procedure or methods of analysis, and the proposed treatment of the findings. (Whereas such a statement is often included in the introductory section(s) of small research papers, in an experimental thesis a separate chapter on design is more usually devoted to these aspects.)

Main Body of the Report

Because of the diversity of research topics and written assignments within separate disciplines, it is not possible to specify directions for organising the main body of a paper or thesis. However, certain general principles should be followed:

(a) Organise the presentation of the argument or findings in a logical and orderly way, developing the aims stated or implied in the introduction.
(b) Substantiate arguments or findings.
(c) Be accurate in documentation.

In both assignments and theses, every effort should be made to write clearly and forcefully within a logical framework.

Conclusion

The conclusion serves the important function of tying together the whole assignment or thesis. In summary form, the developments of the previous chapters should be succinctly restated, important findings discussed, and conclusions drawn from the whole study. In addition, the writer may list unanswered questions that have occurred during the study, and which require further research beyond the limits of the project being reported. The conclusion should leave the reader with the impression of completeness and of positive gain. As with the introduction, the conclusion need not be a separate chapter or section in a small assignment. In a thesis, it usually forms a separate chapter called *Conclusion(s)*, or some alternative descriptive term that gives finality to the study.

Reference Material

A reference section containing details of works consulted or referred to during a study follows the final section of a paper or the last chapter of a thesis. Also appended are certain materials that are important for a full understanding of a study but which, perhaps because of their length, may detract from the main argument if placed in the body of a report. If an index (that is, an alphabetic listing of key terms and concepts in a report) is included, it follows the list of references.

References

The list of references follows the main body of the text and is a separate, but integral, part of a report or thesis. It may be preceded by a division sheet or introduced by a centred capitalised heading REFERENCES. Pagination is continuous and follows the page numbers in the text. In many disciplines, a strong preference exists to list only works cited or referred to in assignments and theses. A bibliography, by contrast, commonly includes works consulted in addition to works to which specific reference is made in the main text. The heading BIBLIOGRAPHY is then used in place of REFERENCES.

In compiling a bibliography, the research student may wish to subdivide the sources consulted in a number of ways. For example, the student may wish to subdivide works into primary and secondary sources. Where such a subdivision occurs, it is usual to centre a major heading under BIBLIOGRAPHY (see Figure 8.11).

BIBLIOGRAPHY

A Primary Sources

The Advertiser, 1858-1900.

The South Australian Register, 1850–1900.

Sinnett, F. *An Account of the Colony of South Australia*, London: Robert K. Burt, 1862.

. . .

B Secondary Sources

Adamson, J.W. *English Education 1789–1902*, Cambridge: Cambridge University Press, 1930.

. . .

Figure 8.11 Bibliography with subdivisions for primary and secondary sources

It is not normal to have subdivisions for a list of references.

Appendix

It is usual to include in an appendix such matters as original data, tables not appearing in the body of the thesis that present supporting evidence, tests that have been constructed by the research student, parts of documents or any supporting evidence that would detract from the major line of argument and would make the body of the text unduly large and poorly structured. Each appendix should be clearly separated from the next and listed in the table of contents (see the sample Table of Contents in Table 8.5). Although the plural form *Appendices* is seen, the preferred Australian form where there is more than one appendix is *Appendixes*.

Index

An index is not required for a written assignment or for an unpublished thesis. If a thesis is subsequently published as a book, monograph or bulletin, an index is necessary for any work of complexity.

The Final Product

From the outset, the student should strive for writing of high quality. The text should be free of errors and untidy corrections. Spelling and grammar check computer programs can help with this task (see Chapter 5). Paper of standard size (usually A4) and of good quality should be used. At an early stage, students should familiarise themselves with the regulations of the institution concerning the submission of theses, noting the requirements relating to:

* number of copies to be submitted (bound and unbound)
* method of binding to be used
* colour of the cloth required for the cover
* lettering that should appear on the spine and front cover.

Methods of Reproduction

The student should consider how the final copy of the thesis is to be produced. For the kinds of reasons advanced in Chapter 5, the use of a word processor is most efficient, not only for the final copy but for earlier drafts as well. Graphs and line drawings can be designed using suitable graphics software and incorporated within a word processing document. The use of a desktop publishing program, in conjunction with a word processor, provides further control over the final appearance of any document.

The assignment or thesis can be printed on a dot matrix or ink jet printer or, for even higher quality, on a laser printer. From the original printed copy, further copies can be made using a photocopier. Sufficient time needs to be scheduled for typing, checking, correcting, collating and, in the case of theses, binding.

Proofreading and Collating

The final draft should be checked very carefully. Spelling, punctuation, tables, figures and setting out must be verified. This is a substantial task requiring considerable patience and diligence. Good research can be marred by errors not detected in the proofreading stage. Corrections must be checked for accuracy. Copies are then collated and checked again to ensure that pages are in proper sequence before submission.

Chapter 9

PAGE AND
CHAPTER FORMAT

Because of the length of a thesis, it is common practice to divide it into chapters and, within each chapter, subdivide the text into sections. Topics then may be addressed separately within chapters. To guide the reader through the document, different level headings are used (with corresponding entries in the table of contents). This chapter details the various options for using headings with accompanying examples. Matters of formatting and style such as margins, spacing, pagination, paragraph indentation and justification also are addressed. Where measurements are given, the units follow the International System of Units used in Australia. Thus for page layout, units are expressed in centimetres (cm), though many word processors also allow inches, points and picas.

Chapter Divisions and Subdivisions

In the interests of readability and ease of reference, chapters of theses are usually divided into sections and subsections. This practice is not always necessary in the shorter assignment or term paper.

The method of indicating chapter divisions and subdivisions depends on the number of such divisions to be made. The kinds of headings employed include centred headings, side headings and paragraph headings. In addition, each chapter has a chapter number and chapter heading. Conventionally, centred headings are used for major divisions and side and paragraph headings for further subdivisions.

Levels of Headings

Many combinations of headings may be used. Modern word processors and printers (see Chapter 5 for details) permit considerable variety in the style of headings adopted. The use of upper case, title case (key words capitalised) and sentence case (first word capitalised), plus the use of bold-face and italics, indicate the hierarchy of headings. The use of underlining is not recommended, nor is it necessary to change fonts.

For most purposes, no more than five levels of headings are needed, and this includes the chapter heading. As with other matters of style, consistency of use is a prime consideration. The following examples illustrate three, four and five levels of headings.

Five Levels

Level 1   **CENTRED HEADING UPPER CASE IN BOLD**

Level 2   **Centred Heading Title Case in Bold**

Level 3   **Side Heading Title Case in Bold**

Level 4   *Side Heading Title Case in Italics*

Level 5   *Paragraph heading sentence case in italics, ending with full stop.*

Four Levels

Level 1   **CENTRED HEADING UPPER CASE IN BOLD**

Level 2   **Centred Heading Title Case in Bold**

Level 3   **Side Heading Title Case in Bold**

Level 4   *Side Heading Title Case in Italics*

Three Levels

Level 1   **Centred Heading Title Case in Bold**

Level 2   **Side Heading Title Case in Bold**

Level 3   *Side Heading Title Case in Italics*

Fewer Levels

The above examples cover most requirements. If fewer than three levels of subdivision are required, centred and/or side headings can be used. The use of more than five levels tends to confuse by subdividing into parts that are too small. Once a method of headings and subheadings has been adopted, this method should be consistent from chapter to chapter. Certain conventions apply to the printing and spacing of headings, the purpose of which is to maintain a consistent format.

Chapter Headings

Each chapter begins on a new page. This applies even if the last page of the preceding chapter has only two or three lines. Chapters are identified by a number and a title.

The chapter designation with number is printed in capitals and arabic numerals with no punctuation, and is usually centred horizontally about 5 cm from the top of the page. The chapter title is also printed in capitals with no final punctuation. It, too, is centred horizontally one double space below the chapter number. Additional spacing (triple) normally separates the chapter title from the text following (see Figure 9.1).

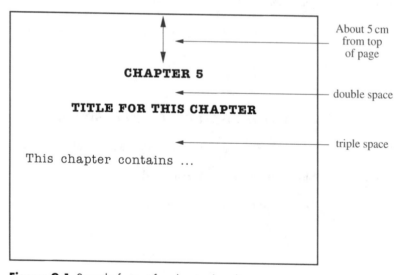

Figure 9.1 Sample format for chapter headings

The chapter designation and title are Level 1 headings as described in the five and four level headings on page 95.

Centred Headings

Centred headings are used for major chapter divisions. Since division implies more than one, there must be at least two major divisions in a chapter before centred headings are necessary. The heading is centred horizontally on the page and printed in lower case except for the initial letter of key words. It may be numbered for purposes of referencing but this is optional. Normally three single spaces separate the centred heading from text above and below. No period follows centred headings.

Side Headings

Side headings, if used with centred headings, indicate further subdivisions; if used without centred headings, side headings indicate major chapter divisions. The side heading is printed flush with the left margin. Numbering is optional. Lower case lettering is used except for the initial letter of key words. Three single spaces normally separate the side heading from text above and one double space from the text below. Again, no period follows side headings.

Paragraph Headings

Paragraph headings are used to indicate divisions within subdivisions, and are often printed in italics and aligned with the left margin. Headings are typed in sentence case (i.e. only the first word and proper nouns are capitalised), and ended with a full stop to separate them from the paragraph beginning on the same line. Spacing follows that used for the rest of the text.

A Note Regarding Headings

All headings should be captions, not sentences. Therefore, no terminal punctuation is used except for paragraph headings where a full stop serves as a separator. Each heading should be brief, yet informative — a statement rather than a question. Headings should not be essential for continuity. A good test is if the sense remains clear when headings are removed. The first sentence following a heading should not depend on the heading for its meaning.

Formatting and Style

Besides chapter divisions and subdivisions, other formatting and style concerns relate to margins, spacing, pagination, paragraph indentation and justification.

Margins

The usual margins recommended are 2.5 cm at the top, bottom and right side of the page, and 4 cm at the left of the page. The wider margin at the left is to allow for binding. These margins give a balanced appearance to the whole. Most word processors make it easy to specify standard margins for all pages.

Spacing

The body of text is normally double spaced, though longer theses sometimes use space and a half. Convention requires different spacing for quotations, footnotes, tables and figures, and appendixes. These special requirements are outlined in the relevant chapters that follow.

Pagination

Every page in an assignment or thesis is given a number, although not every page has its page number printed on it. There are two separate series of page numbers. The preliminaries are numbered using small roman numerals (i, ii, iii, and so on). The title page is assigned the number i although this number is not printed. Page numbers of the preliminaries normally appear at the bottom of the page without punctuation, are centred, and positioned approximately 1.5 cm from the bottom of the page.

All other pages, beginning with the first page of Chapter 1 and including pages of tables and figures, references and appendixes, are numbered with arabic numerals. This number normally appears without punctuation in the top right-hand corner of the page approximately 1.5 cm from the top and aligned with the text 2.5 cm in from the right-hand edge of the paper; or it may be centred at the bottom of the page like the preliminary pages. The exception is the first page of each chapter; like the title page, this may have no page number appearing or, if a page number is printed, it is centred about 1.5 cm from the bottom of the page. Most word processors allow placement of page numbers to be specified easily.

Paragraph Indentation

Formatting styles change as does language usage. It is quite common now not to indent paragraphs (newspapers are an exception) but to provide additional spacing between paragraphs. It is unnecessary both to indent paragraphs and to have additional spacing between paragraphs. See Chapter 10 for indenting quotations and Chapter 11 for indenting footnotes.

Justification of Text

The use of word processors makes it easy to justify text (i.e. have straight edges on both left and right sides as in Figure 9.2). There is some evidence that a ragged right edge or unjustified text (see Figure 9.3) is easier to read. Unless there are institutional specifications, it is optional for text to be fully justified.

The use of word processors makes it easy to justify text (i.e. have straight edges on both left and right sides as in Figure 9.2). There is some evidence that a ragged right edge or unjustified text (see Figure 9.3) is easier to read. Unless there are institutional specifications, it is optional for text to be fully justified.

Figure 9.2 Justified text

The use of word processors makes it easy to justify text (i.e. have straight edges on both left and right sides as in Figure 9.2). There is some evidence that a ragged right edge or unjustified text (see Figure 9.3) is easier to read. Unless there are institutional specifications, it is optional for text to be fully justified.

Figure 9.3 Unjustified text

Sample Thesis Page

Figure 9.4 demonstrates some of the formatting features detailed in this chapter as well as illustrating characteristics of good reporting style. For illustrative purposes, the excerpt is very much abbreviated. The chapter head is a level 1 heading. Within the chapter are four subdivisions, indicated by a centred heading, two styles of side headings and a paragraph heading respectively.

One and a half spacing is used. Since the sample page illustrated in Figure 9.4 opens a chapter, the page number is centred at the bottom of a new page. There is no paragraph indentation and the text is justified.

Each chapter division or subdivision contains a brief introduction. The opening paragraph, for instance, provides an introduction to the whole chapter foreshadowing the major chapter divisions (*Restatement of Problem, Development of Hypotheses*, and so on). The paragraph on *Development of Hypotheses* anticipates two headings, one of which, *Effects of Noise* is shown. The paragraph accompanying *Effects of Noise* foreshadows the subheadings that follow (*Kind of Noise* and *Noise Frequency*), while the paragraph on *Kind of Noise* foreshadows, in turn, the next two sub-sub-headings (*Deletions of different parts* and *Deletions of different lengths*). Students who adopt this kind of writing style will never have two headings that are immediately adjacent: there always will be intervening text acting as an advance organiser for readers. Not only does this kind of writing assist the writer to achieve a more logical organisation, it also helps the reader to grasp the various threads of the argument being presented.

CHAPTER 4

EXPERIMENTAL DESIGN

This chapter commences with a restatement of the problem and the development of hypotheses. The selection of subjects and the test measures are described next followed by ...

Restatement of Problem

The present study was concerned with two aspects of cloze procedure applied to English as a foreign language ...

Development of Hypotheses

The hypotheses were grouped according to whether the focus centred on the effects of noise or on aspects of messages and receivers...

Effects of Noise

Distortion or noise, in terms of the proposed theoretical model, is the interruption of the coded message by deletion of its parts before it is received. There are different kinds of noise and noise can vary in frequency...

Kind of Noise

One method of varying noise is to use blanks of different lengths. Another kind of noise is to delete different parts of ...

Deletions of different lengths. The question of length of blank has practical as well as theoretical significance ....

Deletions of different parts. Different parts of the message that may be deleted include ...

Noise Frequency

The ratio of the number of deletions to total number of words is an index of ...

123

Figure 9.4 Sample page from beginning of chapter

Chapter 10

THE USE OF
QUOTATIONS

While examining the research literature, particularly when photocopying and taking notes, the research student may copy extracts from sources verbatim with the intention that these extracts may be incorporated into a final written report. Although in the initial information gathering stage it is common to accumulate an abundance of appropriate possible quotations from which to choose, it is essential when writing the final report that quotations be selected judiciously and used sparingly. Over-quoting can often be equated with poorly integrated argumentation. The essential selection criterion to follow is relevance whereas the basic mechanical consideration is length of quotation. Long quotations are rarely justified and may cause readers to forget whose ideas they are assessing.

The ability to cite the work of others appropriately is a major indicator of scholarly writing. This chapter discusses when and what to quote, and it details conventions to follow in quoting the work or ideas of others.

When to Quote

Although the final decision of when to quote depends on the problem being investigated and on the judgement of the research student, certain guidelines may assist the student in reaching a decision:

1. Direct quotations should be used only when the original words of the author are expressed so concisely and convincingly that the student cannot improve on these words. Then, the words in the quotation add force, even *punch*, to the research paper or thesis.

2. Direct quotations may be used for documentating a major argument where a footnote would not suffice. In this case, quotations are limited in length and comprise only essential passages.
3. Direct quotations may be used when the student wishes to comment upon, refute or analyse ideas expressed by another writer.
4. Direct quotations may be used when changes, through paraphrasing, could cause misunderstanding or misinterpretation, for instance in citing the words of the law, in stating assumptions underlying a statistical procedure, or in quoting extracts from *Hansard* (Parliamentary Debates) or other official government publications.
5. Direct quotations should be used when citing mathematical, scientific and other formulae.
6. For unpublished material, it is not necessary to obtain permission to quote. If, however, a thesis is to be published, certain copyright problems arise and it is normal practice first to request the publisher's and the author's permission.

Reference is made in Chapter 2 to the necessity of acknowledging the ideas of others where these have been incorporated in an essay or thesis. Failure to do so appropriately is to be guilty of possible plagiarism. The use of direct quotations is one way to acknowledge indebtedness; other ways are through footnotes (see Chapter 11) and referencing (see Chapter 13).

What to Quote

Although there is some flexibility in deciding when to quote, more stringent conventions apply to what is quoted:

1. The exact words of an author or the exact words from an official publication must be quoted. *Exact* means using the *same words*, the *same punctuation*, the *same spelling*, the *same capitalisation*. Extreme care must be taken to reproduce quotations exactly. Complete accuracy is essential.
2. If the tense of a quotation does not fit the context in which it is inserted, if a non-specific pronoun is used for example, and on other occasions as necessary, interpolations may be used in quoted material. However, every interpolation must be enclosed in square brackets, not parentheses, to indicate that words in the original document have been changed or that words have been added.
3. Where a quotation is very long, or where a student wants to use only selected portions, it is permissible to omit sections of an original passage. This procedure is called *ellipsis*. It should be used with extreme care so that the tone, meaning and intention of the original extract are not altered. To indicate ellipsis, three spaced full stops are inserted.

How to Quote

The conventions adopted by different departments vary, but unless given specific directions to the contrary, there are certain general procedures to follow when quoting.

Short Quote vs. Long Quote

The basic form of a quotation is initially determined by its length.

Short Quotation (up to about three lines)

Where a quotation is short – there are no fixed rules but up to about three lines in length – it is common to incorporate the quotation into a sentence or paragraph framework without disrupting the flow of the text. Use double quotation marks at the beginning and the end of the quotation and adopt the same spacing as the rest of the text (that is, double or one and a half line spacing):

> It is clear that society today depends heavily on computer-based technologies and will continue increasingly to do so. As the chairman of one of the world's major airlines noted, "by bits and bytes the world has become computerised over the last fifty years".

It is possible to acknowledge the above quotation in several ways. One way is to place a numbered superscript at the end of the quotation:

> ... "by bits and bytes the world has become computerised over the last fifty years".[1]

The source of the quotation then is provided in a footnote (see Chapter 11 for footnoting conventions). Note that there is no spacing between the period and the footnote number.

A second way to acknowledge the quotation is to place a number in square brackets following the quote and then to list the source in a list of references ordered by cited number:

> ... "by bits and bytes the world has become computerised over the last fifty years".[1]

A third, much more widely used and more direct method of acknowledging the quotation is to use a citation in the text that points forward to a list of references:

> ... "by bits and bytes the world has become computerised over the last fifty years"
> (Ferguson 1991, p. 67).

Readers then may refer to a list of references, ordered alphabetically at the end of the work, for the source of the quotation. Note that the citation is enclosed in parentheses followed by a period, thus linking the citation to the sentence where it belongs. There is no punctuation between name and date and, where a page reference is given, a comma follows the date. The abbreviation for page (p.) is used or, if the quotation extends over two pages, the abbreviation for pages (pp.).

This third method of acknowledging quotations is referred to as the *author-date system* (and sometimes the *Harvard system* after Harvard University where the system gained prominence in the 1930s). Because the author-date system is increasingly used in scholarly writing, further examples are given of its use in citing the work of others. Its use in references is described further in Chapter 13.

If reference is to a specific volume of a work using the author-date system of citation, the volume, and page number too if appropriate, are included within the parentheses:

Ferguson (1991, Vol. 2, p. 67) noted ...

Yet another way of acknowledging the quotation above, also part of the author-date system, is to place the author's name in the text followed by the date (and page number as appropriate) in parentheses:

As Ferguson (1991, p. 67), chairman of one of the world's major airlines noted, "by bits and bytes the world has become computerised over the last fifty years".

Where reference is to an author's work, but not to a specific page or volume, the author's name is followed just by the date. The alternatives in the author-date system are:

(Ferguson 1991)   or   Ferguson (1991)

If there is more than one author, all are included in the citation:

(Ferguson and Clark 1991)
   or
Ferguson and Clark (1991)

Because it is cumbersome to list all names with multiple authors, the usual practice with four or more names is to use the abbreviation for *and others* (et al.):

(Ferguson et al. 1991)
   or
Ferguson et al. (1991)

Sometimes reference is made to different works. The citation then becomes:

(Ferguson 1991; Clark 1991)
(Ferguson 1991; Ferguson 1992)
    or
Ferguson (1991) and Clark (1991)
Ferguson (1991, 1992)

If reference is to works by the same author published within the same year, the different works are distinguished by the letters a, b, c ... after the date:

(Ferguson 1991a; Ferguson 1991b)

On occasion, an author may not be stated. If the work is a book, the title of the work takes the place of the author; if the work is a newspaper article, the newspaper replaces the author:

Politics in Fiji (1992) is a ...

It was reported (*Australian* 8 June 1993, p. 24) ...

Long Quotation (usually four or more lines)

The author-date system of acknowledging quotations applies to long quotations as it does to short quotations. Note, however, the following points:
- Use no quotation marks at the beginning and end of a quotation.
- Use single line spacing for the quotation and indent it (usually 1 cm) from the left margin.
- Introduce the quotation appropriately.
  A colon is often added to follow the words of introduction:

The reaction of parents to the experiment was interesting. For a start, all wanted their children to be involved. The class teacher recorded what happened when students took their laptop computers home:

> It was interesting to hear the reactions of students when they first took their units home. One of the biggest problems was finding time to do their homework because everyone wanted to play with the computer. What started out as a curiosity has been an added bonus, in that parents and families have shown an interest in what their

```
children are doing on the units and have
often become more directly involved in their
child's development as a writer. (Cooke 1986,
p. 12)
```

Note that the author-date citation in parentheses follows the final full stop since here it links to the entire quotation, not just the final sentence.

Ellipsis

To avoid long quotations that are not completely relevant, or to extract critical sections from a longer extract, it is possible to omit part of a quotation.

```
Many parents encourage a learning environment at
home ... and the advertisements of computer
companies, often directed at parents, boldly claim
better opportunities and higher grades for students
who have their own computers. (Hancock 1997,
pp. 44–45)
```

The omission of words is indicated by ellipsis (three full stops). Ellipses can occur at any point within quoted text. If words are omitted at the end of a sentence, the modern practice is to indicate ellipsis again by three full stops.

```
The specification of a simple computer programming
language consists in specifying three components:
(a) a set of primitives ... (b) a set of general flow
charts; and (c) a computation process ...
(Barr 1995, p. 7)
```

If ellipsis is used, it is important not to alter the meaning of the original in any way. The omission of the word *not*, for instance, by the insertion of ... which is very indefinite as to length of omitted material, completely changes an author's meaning. There are certain ethics of quoting and such an omission would seriously violate these.

Interpolations

When it is considered necessary to insert an explanation or correction into a quotation, the convention requires any such editorial change to be placed in square brackets, never parentheses.

Sic

A common interpolation is the inclusion of *sic* after an error in a quotation. In this way the research student indicates that what might be considered an error in reproducing a quotation is an integral part of the original.

> The theory of ferroelectric domains has not been worked out but the theory of ferromagnetic domains is well understood, although modification to provide for charge neutralisation and high electromachanical [sic] coupling is required before it could be applied to ferroelectrics. (Kautsky 1994, p. 26)

Here, the inclusion of *sic* indicates that the research student realises that *electromachanical* is misspelt and should be *electromechanical*.

Comment

If a comment is necessary within a quotation to clarify a point, interpolation may again be used:

> Cobalt, an hexagonal crystal, exemplifies anisotropy energy. The direction of the hexagonal axis is the direction of easy magnetisation [at room temperature], while all directions in the basal plane, normal to the axis, are hard directions. (Robertson 1995, p. 223)

The function of the interpolation here is to specify conditions of temperature and to avoid inaccuracy or error in interpretation.

Supplying an Antecedent

When a non-specific pronoun occurs within a quotation, it is permissible to clarify the issue by inserting the appropriate word or words in square brackets.

> He [William Shakespeare] was undoubtedly the greatest dramatist to date. No other dramatist has rivalled his ability to portray characters with such liveliness and colour. (Snewin 1996, p. 276)

Special Quotations

In a number of disciplines, special problems in quoting can arise. Some of these are indicated below as a guide to developing a consistent pattern of quoting material.

Quote within Quotes

If a quotation occurs within a short extract being quoted, the usual procedure is to enclose the whole quotation within double quotation marks and the internal quotation in single quotation marks:

> Hoggart (1983) has depicted vividly the stereotype attributed to the upper-class by the lower-class in terms of "the ideas of the group, 'acting posh', 'giving y'self airs', 'getting above y'self'..."

If, however, the quotation is long, it is usual to indent the quotation in the normal way without using quotation marks and to use double quotation marks for any internal quotes:

> In discussing equipment required by an Examinations Agency, Keeves (1996, p. 54) notes that:
>
> > Desk-top publishing equipment is today so versatile, that skilled staff can prepare "camera ready" copy relatively easily. Moreover, facilities are now available for the drawing of high quality and detailed diagrams using a desk-top computer, provided the staff have the necessary skills.

Quoting Poetry

The method used to quote poetry depends on the length of the quotation: a short quotation (a line or part of a line) is enclosed in double quotation marks and runs into the text:

> It is easy to feel the mystique of the songs of Ireland through the sound of "thrush, linnet, stare, and wren".

If two lines are quoted, a slash (/) may be used to separate the lines:

> Synge sensed the inevitability of death when he said, "There'll come a season when you'll stretch/ Black boards to cover me".

In longer poetry quotations, quotation marks are not needed; lines are single spaced and indented. Between stanzas, there is a double space:

Something of this power can be felt in Synge's "A Question" where he says:
I asked if I got sick and died, would you
With my black funeral go walking too,
If you'd stand close to hear them talk or pray
While I'm let down in that steep bank of clay.

And, No, you said, for if you saw a crew
Of living idiots pressing round that new
Oak coffin – they alive, I dead beneath
That board – you'd rave and rend them with your
teeth.

Quoting Speech

In some instances, there may be a need to quote the actual words of a speaker or the results of a personal interview. Great care needs to be taken to avoid inaccuracies or the possibility of misrepresentation or misinterpretation. If possible, the extracts should be submitted to the author for approval.

Professor Olim, in his inaugural address delivered at Charles Sturt University, April, 1995, stated, "There can be little doubt that modern society is harnessed to an expanding scientific and technological enterprise."

An alternative method of quoting direct speech acknowledges the source in a footnote:

The increasing demand for a scientifically trained labour force is linked with societal developments, as is illustrated by the following statement: "There can be little doubt that modern society is harnessed to an expanding scientific and technological enterprise."[1]

---

[1] Professor J. Olim of Charles Sturt University, in an inaugural address, April, 1995. Permission to quote secured.

Quotations in Footnotes

When a quotation occurs in a footnote, whether it is incorporated in a sentence or indented and set off from the body of a footnote, double quotation marks are always used:

---

[1] This method was also used by Garibaldi who said, "What is life without supreme sacrifice?"

Indirect Quotations or Paraphrases

To avoid excessively long quotations, it is sometimes necessary to paraphrase a writer's words. The ideas are not enclosed in quotation marks but must still be acknowledged.

Patrick White was different from ordinary people, and this explains how even his friends often felt inadequate in his company. They could not respond to his needs and in that sense they failed him. (Clark 1991, p. 12)

In some cases, where a paraphrase contains controversial viewpoints or the starting point for a detailed analysis, a page reference may be included following the author and date, in the same way that page numbers are given for direct quotes.

Acknowledge Sources and Quote Accurately

The use of quotations varies across disciplines. In Mathematics, for instance, quotations are more sparingly used than in History. Between disciplines there also are minor differences in conventions for quoting. Students need to be aware of practices in the discipline within which they are writing.

The most important message from this chapter is the necessity to acknowledge sources of information and quote accurately. For all disciplines, it is essential to refer to the work of others, if only to indicate the context of a particular study. Reference may be made by quoting excerpts from authors' writings (more common in some disciplines than others) or by citing publications of researchers. Chapter 13 deals with conventions of referencing in lists of references.

FOOTNOTES

Footnotes are conventional procedures used in scholarly writing to validate or to explain certain aspects in the main text. Such devices should be used sparingly and only when the material being presented clearly needs amplification or acknowledgment. Footnotes should appear only in the body of a paper or thesis, never in an abstract. Footnotes can be distracting if they are so numerous and frequent that they persistently impinge upon the reader's attention. Therefore, it becomes essential, before including any footnotes in a paper or essay, to assess whether the material being relegated to a footnote is important enough to be incorporated into the main body of the text, or whether it is essential to include it at all. Once a decision is reached on this point, a number of guidelines can be followed for appropriate footnoting.

Use of Footnotes

Two kinds of footnotes in text are commonly employed. One kind is for scholarly honesty to acknowledge sources and authorities. Such footnotes often:

- validate a point, statement or argument
- acknowledge a direct quotation or indirect quotation
- provide readers with sufficient information to consult sources independently.

Information in footnotes of this kind where sources and authorities are acknowledged includes:

1. the source of information, usually the name of the author
2. the title of the source
3. the exact page(s) of the source of reference

4. the date of publication
5. the publisher and place of publication (optional).

The second kind of footnote is to include additional content that is not strictly relevant to the main argument but yet is too important to be omitted. Such footnotes may:

- explain, supplement, or amplify material that is included in the main body of a paper
- provide cross-references to other sections of a paper.

In those fields of study where the author-date system of referencing is employed (see Chapters 10 and 13), footnotes of the first kind to acknowledge sources and authorities are not used; even footnotes of the second kind for including additional content are rare.

To avoid footnotes that contain long or complex material, it is often preferable to state in the body of the text that the reader can refer to an Appendix:

    Appendix A contains a copy of the interview
    schedule.

Placement of Footnotes

As the name implies, footnotes are usually found at the foot of a page, although in some manuscripts they appear at the end of each chapter or at the end of the paper (and are then called *endnotes*). When placed at the end of a paper or chapter, a centred heading *Endnotes* is required. In this chapter the term *footnotes* is used regardless of placement.

Reference to footnotes is made using superscripts (that is, numerals raised above the baseline) in the body of the text where the particular reference is given. There is generally less interruption to the text if the superscript is placed at the end of the sentence in which the reference has been made. However, such a procedure may not always be clear, in which case the superscript should follow immediately the word or phrase to which reference is made. With quotations, the footnote reference is always placed at the end of the quotation. The superscript appears without any punctuation and without any space intervening between it and the preceding word or punctuation mark.

When footnotes are placed at the foot of the page, no heading is used. Instead, they are commonly separated from the text by a short solid line called a *separator*. The separator is approximately 3.5 cm long, drawn from the left-hand margin and one double space below the last line of the text.

    Among certain of the tribes of North-West
    America[1], a surplus in wealth and leisure time,

combined with skill in craftsmanship, fostered
the development of potlatching where symbolic
forms of wealth and values were distributed and
manipulated to obtain prestige. Prestige resulted
from publicly disposing of wealth, not in
accumulating it.[2]

---

[1] For example, Haida, Kwakiutl, Tlingit and Nootka.

[2] G. Lienhardt. 1966. *Social Anthropology*. Oxford
University Press, Oxford, p. 89.

Format of Footnotes

The recommended practice is to indent the first line of the footnote in the
same way as paragraphs. If paragraphs are indented, footnotes are
indented by the same amount; if paragraphs are flush left, footnotes also
are flush left. Footnotes occupying more than one line are single spaced. A
double space separates successive footnotes.

Footnotes are usually numbered consecutively throughout a chapter or
continuously through a paper or thesis. In works containing very few footnotes, a new numbering system may begin on each page. In mathematical
and scientific papers and theses, where arabic numerals may be confusing,
special symbols such as asterisks and daggers (*, †) are often used.

Conventions in Footnoting

Certain conventions are followed in footnoting:
1. In the first footnote referring to each source, it is usual to give the full
   name of the author in its normal order – that is author's initials or given
   name, followed by surname.
2. In citing reference details, the usual bibliographical procedures are
   followed:
   (a) *Books*
      For books, the author's name, title of complete work (usually itali-
      cised), publisher, place of publication, year of publication and page
      numbers are cited:

---

[1] Janet Turner Hospital, *The Last Magician*,
University of Queensland Press, St. Lucia, 1992,
p. 125.

(b) *Journal articles*

In the case of journal articles, the author's name, title of article, name of periodical (usually italicised), volume and/or issue number, year of publication and page numbers are cited:

---

[1] R. Kerr, Taking shots at ozone hole theories, *Science*, 14, 1986, p. 67.

---

3. After the first reference is detailed in a footnote, it is not necessary to repeat the name of the author, publisher and other details in subsequent footnotes. Accepted abbreviations to avoid repetitious and lengthy documentation are the use of:

(a) *ibid.*

If reference is made to a different page of a source supplied immediately above, it is possible to use the term *ibid.*

---

[1] Janet Turner Hospital, *The Last Magician*, University of Queensland Press, St. Lucia, 1992, p. 125.

[2] ibid., pp. 147–49.

(b) *loc. cit.*

If reference is made to the same page as a preceding but not immediately preceding reference, the last name of the author and the phrase *loc. cit.* are used:

---

[1] Hudson, loc. cit.

(c) *op. cit.*

If reference is made to the same work as a preceding but not immediately preceding reference, *op. cit.* precedes page reference but follows author's name.

---

[1] Moore, op. cit., p. 238.

---

4. The abbreviation *p.* for page and *pp.* for pages is the acceptable method of citing page references.

Problems in Footnoting

A number of problems may arise in the footnoting of more complex material:

1. Footnotes that are continued over more than one page need to be continued in mid-sentence so that the reader realises additional material is to be found on the bottom of the following page.
2. Footnotes in tables or figures should be placed one single space below the table or figure. A separator is not needed, but a double space is used between footnotes. Where lower case letters are used rather than asterisks or daggers, the lettering is consecutive only for each table or figure, not for the whole paper or thesis.
3. In citing a secondary source, a single footnote is sufficient, but both primary and secondary references should be included:

S. Dillon, Jobs for the girls, quoted in
Millicent E. Poole, *Education and Work*, ACER,
Canberra, p. 134.

An acceptable alternative to *quoted in* is *cited by*.

Points to Remember

Footnotes are like parentheses — something added to the text. The text ought not to depend for its meaning on a footnote. Further points to consider:

1. Decide whether a footnote strengthens or validates a point made in the paper.
2. Include footnotes in the first draft.
3. Check each footnote for accuracy and for correct format.
4. Having adopted a method of footnoting, be consistent throughout the whole assignment or thesis.
5. Footnotes should be concise, but never sacrifice clarity and readability for brevity.
6. Footnotes are normally single-spaced, no matter where they appear in a manuscript.
7. Regardless of length, all footnotes are terminated by a full stop.
8. The same bottom margin should be maintained on each page whatever the number of footnotes.
9. A footnote may continue on consecutive pages. Where a footnote is very long, however, assess whether an appendix might be more appropriate than a footnote.

Many word processors have a footnotes feature. More powerful word processors allow writers to choose footnote reference marks or to have footnotes automatically numbered; to use separators as in the examples above; to include continuation messages for footnotes continuing to another page; and to display footnotes at the bottom of a page or at the end of a paper or chapter. Writers whose research is in a discipline where footnotes are commonly used should look for a footnote facility when choosing a word processor.

Chapter 12

TABLES AND FIGURES

Writers can often help readers' understanding of text by using tables and figures to convey certain information. The use of tables and figures is recommended to present data of different kinds (for instance, earnings, income, temperatures, correlations) or to show the interrelationship of a number of parts (anatomical, spatial, geographical). Their use is not recommended simply to repeat information adequately covered in the text. This chapter illustrates the various uses of tables and figures, their placement in a paper, and conventions and guidelines for numbering, formatting and preparing tables and figures.

Use of Tables and Figures

The word *table* is usually restricted to information presented in a tabular form whereas the term *figure* is used to designate any other illustrative material such as graphs, charts, diagrams, drawings, maps or photographs. Sometimes the term *plate* is used for photographic materials.

A table or figure should not merely repeat information covered in the text but augment it. The text always must contain sufficient detail to sustain the particular argument being put forward. Some readers shy away from a table of numbers and prefer to read the evidence presented. Other readers find a tabular presentation quicker to follow than textual presentation. The same information should not, of course, be presented in both tabular and graphical form. A table of the running speed in seconds of a group of athletes over a hundred metres and a bar graph of the same information would be needlessly repetitive. However, an appendix often contains data on which a figure is based.

It is not always necessary to present data in tabular form if these can be presented more simply in the body of the text. For example, the following is clear and unambiguous:

The 423 participants ranged from 17 to 20 years and comprised 155 females and 268 males drawn from five faculties.

It is not necessary either to present as a full table (that is, one included in a List of Tables in the Contents) a set of data that is presented in tabular form for simplicity. For example:

The reasons given by volunteers for their initial involvement were substantially the same for both men and women:

To help people and for social concern/ responsibility	41.2%
Because family and friends are in an organisation	22.8%
To develop skills or for social contact	26.7%
Other	9.3%

If, however, the set of data takes up more than about five lines, it is usual to present it as a numbered table.

Placement of Tables and Figures

Tables and figures should always be introduced. Stated another way, the table or figure should always *follow* its first mention in the text. Further, a table or figure should follow its first mention as closely as possible. Typical ways of introducing tables and figures are the following:

Means, standard deviations and standard errors of means are presented in Table 22.

Figure 4 shows the apparatus used in the second experiment.

With a word processor, and particularly with a desktop publishing program, it is usually quite easy to place a table or figure conveniently close to, and following, its first mention in the text. While it is possible to place larger tables and figures on separate pages — and in days gone by when most papers were prepared by typewriter this was the recommended practice — it is more usual now to surround tables and figures by text so that normal margins are maintained. An exception is when preparing a paper for publication. Guidelines for particular journals then need to be followed.

Often a decision must be made whether to include tables in the body of the text or in an appendix. The writer must be guided here according to whether the material being presented is essential for an understanding of the argument or whether the material consists of supporting details to which interested readers may refer if they wish. If the material is essential for the conclusions that follow, it should be presented in the main body of the text. The aim should always be to present a smooth flowing argument or thesis. Incidentally, sufficient information should be provided for the interested reader to rework calculations or to replicate a study. The place for these basic test data, as they are often called, is an appendix.

Numbering of Tables

All tables should be numbered to permit easy identification. One method is to number tables consecutively through a thesis using arabic numerals (Table 1, Table 2, Table 3 ...). Another method is to number tables consecutively within chapters (Table 4.1, Table 4.2, Table 4.3 ... for tables in chapter 4, Table 5.1, Table 5.2, Table 5.3 ... for chapter 5, and so on). If tables are included in an appendix, the numbering sequence continues from the last table number in the text if the first of these methods is used; otherwise, the numbering is consecutive within appendixes (e.g. Table A.1, Table A.2 ... within Appendix A, Table B.1, B.2 ... within Appendix B).

Numbering of Figures

The same conventions for numbering and format of tables apply to figures, with one important exception: the word figure with its appropriate number is placed *below* the figure (see Figures 12.1 and 12.2).

Table and Figure Captions

Every table or figure has a title. In a way the title is a concise summary of what is presented. It is self-contained and usually in caption form (not a complete sentence). The first letter of the first word and proper nouns are capitalised. Unless the caption is a sentence, there is no full stop. The table number and caption are always placed *above* the table, whereas for a figure, the caption is placed *below*. An example of a commonly used format is seen in Table 12.1 which shows a short excerpt from a table. The word *Table* and its number are in boldface; the accompanying caption is aligned with the left hand edge of the table. The whole table (including caption) is separated from the text by a triple space above and below:

Table 12.1 Indices of weekly award rates of pay of full-time adult employees (June 1990 = 100.00)

	NSW	Vic	Qld	SA	WA	Tas
1990	...	...				
1991						

An alternative format (see Table 12.2) sometimes seen is to centre the caption above a table and use full capitals for the word *Table*:

TABLE 12.2

Global primary energy consumption per capita, 1990

Word processors have, however, reduced the need to use capitals as a form of emphasis.

If the length of any caption extends over a line, it is commonly single spaced, and indented so that the second and subsequent lines align with the start of the caption (called a *hanging indent*). The captions in Tables 12.3 and 12.4 feature hanging indents. As with many of the conventions described, consistency should be the aim.

Phrases such as *Table showing* (for instance, *Table showing average rainfall for 1992*) or *Figure showing* are unnecessary and should be avoided. The caption for each table or figure must correspond exactly with that given in the List of Tables or List of Figures.

Format of Tables

The different components of a table are:

1. the table number
2. the caption or title
3. the boxheads — the captions identifying the vertical columns
4. the stub, the first column in the table, identifying the row entries
5. the field, the columns containing data.

Tables should be presented as simply as possible. Table 12.3 illustrates the format of a relatively straightforward table.

Table 12.3 Area of the states and territories of Australia in square kilometres

States/Territories	Area (km^2)
WA	2 515 500
Qld	1 727 200
NT	1 326 200
SA	984 000
NSW	801 600
Vic.	227 600
Tas.	67 800
ACT	2 400
Total	7 682 300

Note the following points:

1. **Table 12.3** (the table number) is aligned with the left of the table and the caption is formatted as a hanging indent.
2. A horizontal line closes the table at the top and bottom.
3. There are no vertical lines. Modern formatting almost completely precludes the use of vertical lines in tables.
4. The boxheads for the stub and field are taken from the caption of the table.
5. The stub (column 1) identifies the states/territories.
6. There is only one field of data (column 2).

Table 12.3 illustrates further desirable features of tables:

1. The units of measurement are stated and, although an abbreviation is used, it is clear since it occurs in the caption for the table.
2. The entries in the stub are arranged so that areas are in descending order of magnitude. This arrangement assists in interpreting the data in the table.
3. The entries in the stub, which consist of words, are left-justified (aligned with the left margin of the table); and the entries in the field, which are numbers, are right justified.
4. The boxhead for the stub and the field have a ruled line below them to function as a separator from the table entries; similarly, the bottom table entry has a ruled line above it to separate it from the state entries from which it differs, representing as it does the total area of the country.

Consistency and simplicity are key criteria in setting out tables. The best guide is to keep the reader constantly in mind: *Does the setting out assist comprehension?*

Table 12.4 illustrates a slightly more complex table. Note the method of presenting sub-sets of data within the one table. This is often preferable to having two separate tables for the same data. The use of an asterisk is a common way of indicating if results in tables are statistically significant. A table should be self-contained and self-explanatory. That is, all information necessary for interpreting the table should be present.

Table 12.4 Significance of differences between deletion rates (every 2nd, 4th, 8th, 16th and 32nd words omitted) for easy and difficult passages, together with means for different deletion rates

	Deletion rates				Means
	2nd	4th	8th	16th	
Easy passages					
2nd					1.50
4th	1.94*				3.44
8th	2.44*	0.50			3.94
16th	2.88*	0.94	0.44		4.38
32nd	3.44*	1.50*	1.00*	0.56	4.94
	Critical difference = 0.951				
Difficult passages					
2nd					1.19
4th	0.81*				2.00
8th	1.25*	0.44			2.44
16th	1.25*	0.44	0.00		2.44
32nd	1.50*	0.69	0.25	0.25	2.69
	Critical difference = 0.808				

* Denotes significant differences at the 0.05 level.

Format of Figures

Much tabular information can be presented alternatively as a chart or graph. The term *figure* encompasses diagrammatic forms of presenting information such as pie graphs, bar charts, column charts, line charts, area charts, scatter plots, time line charts and three-dimensional charts. Besides these diagrammatic forms of presenting information, the term *figure* includes drawings, plans and other diagrams.

The format of figures, like tables, should be as simple as the data presented permit. Figure 12.1 illustrates the setting out of a typical graph, the essential components of which are the figure itself, the figure identification and caption. Note that the figure number and caption appear below the figure. The source of the data on which the figure is based is acknowledged using a special symbol (here the [†] symbol to avoid confusion with the arabic number of the figure) and is set in a smaller font size.

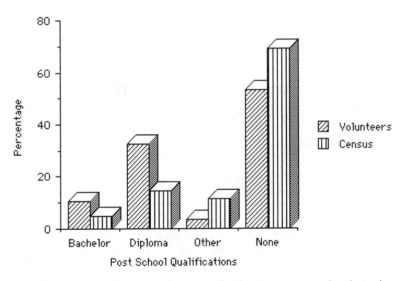

Figure 12.1 Post school qualifications of volunteers compared with similar qualifications held in the general population[†]

[†] Based on data in Noble, J. 1991. *Volunteering: A Current Perspective*, Volunteer Centre of South Australia, Adelaide.

By contrast, Figure 12.2 is a simple line drawing. Again, the source is acknowledged using a special symbol to avoid any confusion with the figure number.

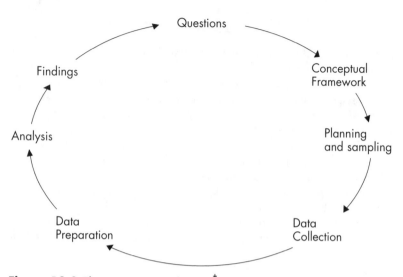

Figure 12.2 The survey research cycle[†]

[†] Source: Rosier, M. J. and Ross, K. N. 1992. Sampling and administration. In J. Keeves (ed.) *The IEA Technical Handbook*, International Association for the Evaluation of Educational Achievement, The Hague.

Preparation of Figures

Before the widespread use of personal computers, the preparation of figures for theses was done manually with black india ink on quality cartridge paper. It was a highly skilled task and students often engaged the services of a graphic artist. For term papers and reports, figures were commonly drawn on graph paper. Nowadays, if students have access to graphics software on a personal computer, the compilation of graphs and drawings becomes a relatively easy task. Nor does one need artistic skills to produce professional looking figures. Most importantly, as with other aspects of producing the final copy of an assignment or thesis, the writer retains control.

Chapter 5 describes some of the electronic tools available to help students prepare figures. Three figures in that chapter (Figures 5.4 to 5.6) and Figures 12.1 and 12.2 in this chapter were all produced using inexpensive graphics software: a graphics program for drawing graphs and a paint program for line drawings.

Examination of Figure 12.1 above highlights features common to many graphs that a good graphics program handles automatically, while at the same time giving the user control over specific elements:

1. The units along the y-axis or vertical scale of the graph (*percentages* in this case) are indicated clearly, as are the categories along the x-axis or horizontal scale (here *post school qualifications*).

2. Users have full control over the captions for both x- and y-axes of graphs: both the wording of captions and their format (the use of plain text, bold, italics, and so on).
3. Wherever practicable, the zero point should be shown on the y-axis of a graph, if necessary by indicating a break on the axis.
4. For some graphs it might be desirable to indicate the heights of the separate columns. This information can be added easily above each column.
5. The contents of the graph are clearly indicated in the accompanying legend which the user may position at will.
6. The particular graphics program used gives a choice of a three-dimensional effect as shown, or a traditional two-dimensional appearance. The user also may choose whether to draw a column graph or a variety of other graphs (bar, area, stack or line).
7. A further option is to close the graph at the top and right hand side or, as here, to elect for an open graph.
8. The figure caption below the graph describes the contents of the graph as well as acknowledging the source of the data on which the graph is based.

Graphics software provides the research student with a powerful set of tools to help in the preparation of many kinds of different figures. What students must aim for are figures that present information as simply as possible, and that can stand alone without the reader needing to refer to the text to understand them.

Footnotes to Tables and Figures

Footnotes are often used with tables and figures to explain a point within a table or figure, or to define an abbreviation or symbol. Letters of the alphabet or special symbols such as * and † are used for referencing rather than arabic numerals as the former are less likely to be confused with table and figure numbers. Footnotes are normally single spaced with one line spacing between footnotes (see Table 12.4 and Figures 12.1 and 12.2 on the previous pages for examples).

Very Large Tables and Figures

There are several methods for dealing with tables or figures too large to fit on one page:
1. The table or figure may be placed sideways (sometimes called *landscape* orientation) on a page.
2. The table or figure may be reduced photographically.

3. The table may be continued over more than one page (usually not applicable to figures). An example is Table 13.1 in the next chapter.
4. The table or figure may be produced on a larger sheet of paper and folded into the report or thesis.

The particular method chosen reflects to some extent thesis style. Nevertheless, the following points in connection with the above methods should be considered before reaching a decision:

1. Generally avoid presenting material sideways on the page if the same material can be presented without readers having to alter their normal reading position. When the page is turned on its side, the table or figure number and caption appear on the spine or binding edge.
2. If photographic facilities are available, and if reduction does not cause difficulties in reading, photographic reduction is a good solution to the very large table or figure.
3. If a graphics program is not available, it is a good technique to draw graphs, diagrams, charts or maps on cartridge paper for subsequent reduction since this smooths blemishes and irregularities and helps to give a polished presentation.
4. Consider whether a large table should not appear in an appendix. If not, the setting out of the second and subsequent pages of a continued table are the same as for the first page of the table except that the word *continued* is used, and the table heading is not repeated. Only the last page of the table is closed at the bottom (that is, contains a single horizontal line across all the columns). For an example of a continued table see Table B.1 in Appendix B.
5. The folding of pages tends to make an assignment or thesis bulky. If folding is used, the page should be folded right over left to a maximum width of 10.5 cm (with the standard 29.5 cm × 21 cm A4 paper). This allows the pages to be trimmed (in the case of binding) without cutting the folded page in two. Unless absolutely necessary, the page should not be folded from the top or from the bottom.

Pagination and Margins

Pages containing tables or figures are numbered as are all pages of an assignment or thesis. The page number should appear in the normal position (for example, the top right-hand corner or bottom centred) even when material is presented sideways on the page or when the page is folded. If normal margins are not maintained, the page number may need to be moved slightly from its normal position.

Where possible, pages containing tables or figures should conform to the normal margins (3.5 cm on the left-hand side and 2.5 cm at top, bottom and right hand side). However, exceptions to this rule include the following:

1. Where tables and figures are spaced one per page, they should be placed in the normal position with respect to the top of the page. Any blank space is left at the bottom of the page.
2. Narrow tables, such as Table 12.3 (page 121), should not be stretched to full width if readability or appearance on the page is impaired as a result.
3. Broad tables or figures may exceed the normal margins but binding and trimming need to be considered carefully.

Spacing and Alignment

Whereas the text of an assignment or thesis is normally double-spaced, this does not necessarily apply to the typing of tables. Single or one and a half spacing may be used. With columns of numbers, it is common to single-space and leave one double space after every fifth or tenth row. The key consideration is ease of reference.

Spacing between columns in a table is governed by the same consideration — ease of reference.

Columns consisting of words are normally left-justified whereas columns of figures are right-justified (see Table 12.3, page 121).

Data containing ± or decimal points are aligned first on the ± and then on the decimal points. A similar procedure is used for data showing a range of values:

$$14.21 \pm 1.3 \qquad 12 \text{ to } 21.3$$
$$1.52 \pm 0.12 \qquad -3.4 \text{ to } -1.2$$
$$312 \pm 12 \qquad -21.8 \text{ to } 111.4$$

Chapter  13

REFERENCING

Mention is made in previous chapters of the need to refer to the work of other researchers in a field, to take notes carefully so that quotes are accurate, and to observe the conventions for quotations and footnotes in the printed text. Chapter 10 describes how to acknowledge sources within text, while this chapter contains details of methods of referencing in bibliographies of assignments and theses. The author-date system, now widely accepted across most (but not all) disciplines, is described, and examples are given for a range of materials to which reference may be made.

Reference Systems

Strictly speaking, a bibliography is a list of published works, although by common usage both published and unpublished materials are listed in a bibliography. There are several different kinds of bibliography.

1. *Works Cited* comprises a list of sources that has been referred to in the text or the footnotes of a paper.
2. *Sources Consulted* is a broader kind of bibliography and consists of a comprehensive listing of works consulted, including those that are not quoted from, referred to or strictly relevant to the subject of a particular paper.
3. A *Selected Bibliography* contains those sources cited, together with the more relevant of the works that have been consulted.
4. A *Brief Annotated Bibliography* is a list of references, at least some of which are followed by a note on the content and usefulness of the references.

The *Works Cited* is the most common form of bibliography, although the heading *Bibliography* or *References* or *List of References* is normally substituted for *Works Cited*. The term *References* is the most commonly used of these terms across different disciplines and is the term used in this book. Whichever term is used, however, the heading is placed, in the case of theses, at the top of a page using a similar format to chapter headings. For assignments, the heading comes at the end of the paper, either following immediately on or commencing a new page. For assignments and theses, each page is numbered following on from the last page of the preceding section (see notes on pagination in Chapter 9). The references are usually placed immediately after the last chapter of a thesis, but some writers prefer to place the references after any appendixes.

Every book, article, thesis, document or manuscript that has been consulted and cited should be included in the list of references. The references should follow a logical arrangement in alphabetical order of author's surname. Current practice in most disciplines favours one comprehensive listing — not a division into primary sources and secondary sources, or books, journals, newspapers, documents and official papers, and manuscripts. In an historical study, however, such an ordering may be required, and then the term usually employed is *Bibliography*.

There are no absolute rules on referencing. The method adopted is influenced by the method of citation in the body of the assignment or thesis, the system of footnoting employed, the practice of a particular field of study, and the requirements of the lecturer setting the assignment or of the institution conferring the degree. Should students find that the format recommended below is not acceptable in all respects, the format prescribed by the institution should be substituted for the one presented here. Nevertheless, students may still find that this chapter contains useful suggestions on many finer points of referencing. The major aim always should be to achieve clarity and consistency and, above all, accuracy in referencing.

Setting out and punctuation in references follow a different format from a footnote. For example, in a footnote the author's name is given in the natural order of initials or first names followed by the surname, but in a list of references the surname precedes the initials of first names. The reason for differences in format lies in the purpose of each system. The purpose of a footnote is to give the specific location of the source of a statement (fact, idea, concept) made in the text, including the number of the actual page on which the statement appears in the original source. Such a practice assists the reader to verify the information readily. The purpose of a bibliographical entry in a list of references, on the other hand, is to identify the whole work rather than a specific part of it. It would be cumbersome to repeat the general reference on each occasion that a source is cited in a footnote, yet the full details of the source need to be included somewhere in the assignment or thesis for readers to consult as required. This is especially important with revised editions (in which case the number of the edition also should be given), or where a work has been republished by another publisher.

Harvard and APA Systems

Two widely adopted forms of referencing, well established in the natural sciences and quite widespread in the social sciences and education, are the Harvard and APA (American Psychological Association) systems.

The Harvard system was developed at Harvard University in the 1930s; it was an adaptation and simplification of referencing conventions in the *Chicago Manual of Style*, first published by the University of Chicago Press in 1906. Characteristic of the Harvard system is the use of author and date as the form of referring to sources in text (see Chapter 10) with authors' works listed alphabetically in a separate list of references. The vastly simplified system, in comparison with the previously almost universal academic practice of footnotes that used Latin abbreviations (op.cit., loc.cit. and ibid.), spread to many academic disciplines. Each edition of the Australian *Style Manual* has given increasing space to the Harvard or author-date system of referencing.

The APA system is a variation of the author-date system presented by the American Psychological Association as a guide to publication. This system also dates from the 1930s and 1940s, and has been promoted through the APA's *Publication Manual*.

Minor and subtle differences exist between the Harvard and APA systems and writers often adopt a mixture of the two. Table 13.1 illustrates some of these differences.

Table 13.1 Differences between the Harvard and APA (American Psychological Association) systems of referencing

Harvard System	APA System
Anderson, J and Poole, M (1998) *Assignment and Thesis Writing*, 3rd ed, John Wiley and Sons, Brisbane	Anderson, J., & Poole, M. (1998) *Assignment and thesis writing*, 3rd ed.). Brisbane: John Wiley & Sons.
no punctuation after initials or date	full stops after initials and dates; for multiple authors, comma separates authors
names joined by *and*	names joined by &
book and journal names in title case*	book names in sentence case[†] journal names in title case

Continued

Harvard System	APA System
commas separate publishing elements	period after title or edition colon after place of publication
edition without brackets or punctuation	edition with brackets and periods
publisher followed by place of publication	place of publication followed by publisher

* Title case uses capitals for the first letters of key words.
† Sentence case uses capitals for the first letter of the first word and for proper nouns.

Author-date System

The Harvard and APA systems have in common the author followed by the date, and it is this author-date system of referencing that now is followed in a majority of disciplines, though commonly there is a mixture of the two systems. A practice adopted by many university departments, supported in part by the Australian *Style Manual*, and followed in this book is to use:

- full stops after initials and date
- *and* to link authors, without a preceding comma where there are just two authors (it seems unnecessary to advocate the use of *and* in textual references and & in a list of references, and the practice in this book is, therefore, to use *and* in both cases)
- no parentheses around date
- title case for book and periodical names
- edition number in brackets
- publisher followed by place of publication (joined by comma)
- normal punctuation rules for abbreviations (see *Abbreviations, Spacing and Capitalisation* in this chapter)

e.g.

Anderson, J. and Poole, M. 1998. *Assignment and Thesis Writing* (3rd ed.). John Wiley and Sons, Brisbane.

Essential Information

Three key kinds of references are to books (authored and edited), journal articles and articles or chapters in edited books.

Book References

Essential information for each book reference has three components:
- name(s) and initials of author(s) together with date of publication
- book title (from a full page, not the spine) including edition if other than the first
- details concerning the imprint (publisher and place of publication).

Each of these three components is followed by a period. In a list of references, it is standard practice to use initials of authors, rather than first names:

> Baker, M., Robertson, F. and Sloan, J. 1993. *The Role of Immigration in the Australian Higher Education Market*. Australian Government Publishing Service, Canberra.

> Wilson, P. 1992. *Trends and Issues in Australian Crime and Criminal Justice*. Australian Institute of Criminology, Canberra.

If a book is edited, the abbreviation *ed.* or *eds* is placed in parentheses following the name of the author(s):

> Wingrove, K. (ed.) 1990. *Norman Lindsay on Art, Life and Literature*. University of Queensland Press, Brisbane.

Journal Article References

In the case of journal articles, the place of publication and the publisher are not included since this information is usually well known, particularly for the more important periodicals. However, the volume number, issue number if used, and the inclusive page numbers for the article are given. The essential information, then, for journal articles also has three components and, as for book references, each component is followed by a full stop:
- name(s) and initials of author(s) together with date of periodical
- title of article
- title of periodical, volume or issue number and page numbers

> Dyson, J. 1993. Shocking behaviour of young stars in Orion. *Nature*, (363), 21–22.

If an issue number is available as well as a volume number, it is placed in parentheses after the volume number:

Hart, G. 1990. Peer consultation in review. *Australian Journal of Advanced Nursing*, 5 (4), 22-27.

Note that for journal articles, page numbers are specified without accompanying abbreviations (*p.* or *pp.*).

Articles or Chapters in Edited Works

Where reference is made to a chapter or article in an edited book, both the author and title of the chapter or article, together with the editor and other details of the book, are included in the one bibliographical entry. Essential information for such entries has three components, each followed by a full stop:

- name(s) and initials of author(s) together with date of edited work
- title of chapter or article
- name(s) of editor(s), title of edited work, publisher and place of publication

Optionally, page numbers of a chapter or article are added after the title of the edited work.

The third component is preceded by the word *In* which serves to link all its sub-parts together:

Slee, R. 1991. Institutional approaches to discipline. In M. Lovegrove and R. Lewis, (eds) *Classroom Discipline*, Longman Cheshire, Melbourne.

Trabasso, T., Secco, T. and Van den Broek, P. 1984. Causal cohesion and story coherence. In H. Mandl, N.L. Stein and T. Trabasso (eds) *Learning and Comprehension of Text*, Erlbaum, Hillsdale, NJ.

Note that the initials of editors precede their names since this information is not used to order reference entries alphabetically. The date cited in the list of references is the date of the edited work (not necessarily the date of the original article) since the edited work is listed as the source of information. Where a city may not be well known, place of publication sometimes includes state (usually abbreviated) as well as city.

Abbreviations, Spacing and Capitalisation

Abbreviating periodical names is generally to be avoided since confusion may result with little saving of space. Certain abbreviations listed in Table 13.2 are, however, acceptable for additional information about publications.

Table 13.2 Abbreviations in referencing and their use

Abbreviated Form	Full Form	Use
ed.	edition, edited, editor	
eds	editors	for edited works
2nd ed.	second edition	
3rd ed.	third edition	
rev. ed.	revised edition	
p.	page	for newspaper but not journal articles
pp.	pages	for newspaper but not journal articles
Vol.	Volume	for volume number
vols	volumes	for number of volumes

The general rule for punctuation is to follow the abbreviated form with a full stop if the final letter is not the same as the final letter of the full form.

Single-spaced entries for references, with double spacing between entries, give a readable format. Names of authors stand out more clearly if references are entered using what is called a hanging indent. That is, indent the second and subsequent lines of each entry about 0.5 cm as illustrated in all the sample references in this chapter.

For annotated entries, the annotation starts on a new line indented by the same amount (0.5 cm) as hanging indents:

Jones, B. 1995. *Sleepers, Wake! Technology and the Future of Work* (4th ed.). Oxford University Press, Melbourne.

Former Minister of Science, Barry Jones, urges Australians to consider the impact of technology on society and think seriously about the future of work.

In a list of references, title case is used for book titles (that is, capitalise all key words) and titles are italicised, or underlined where italics is unavailable. No italics or underlining is used for unpublished works. If a reference comprises more than one volume, the entry must state the total number of volumes comprising the reference:

Jessop, J.P. and Toelken, H.R. (eds) 1986. *Flora of South Australia* (4 vols). South Australian Government Printing Division, Adelaide.

In the case of journal articles, the titles of journals are italicised and in title case. Titles of journal articles are in sentence case (that is, capitalise only first word, proper nouns and first word after a colon):

Winne, P.H., Graham L. and Prock, L. 1993. A model of poor readers' text-based inferencing: Effects of explanatory feedback. *Reading Research Quarterly*, 28 (1), 52-66.

Alphabetical and Chronological Order

To locate references quickly in an alphabetically ordered list of references, author's names always appear with initials following the name (though in all other cases such as names of editors and translators, initials precede the name). The determination of a strict alphabetical order can sometimes still be a problem. Note that Mc and Mac are listed under M as though the prefix were spelled Mac; and surnames starting with St are treated as though they were given in full (that is, Saint). The simple way to treat names such as de Jong, D'Orsogna, Le Thomas is to order them alphabetically starting with the first letter of the prefix. If in doubt, a telephone book or electoral role may be a helpful guide.

In the case of compound surnames such as P.L. Ferguson-Smith, the name becomes Ferguson-Smith, P.L. and is placed in alphabetical order beginning with the initial letter of the first part of the surname. Initials help alphabetical ordering where names are identical:

Farraday, N.

Ferguson, J.

Ferguson, W.S.

Ferguson-Smith, P.L.

Ferguson-Stuart, W.

Fordson, V.

Some authorities state that, where there is more than one author of a particular publication, it is only necessary to reverse the surname and initials of the first (senior) author of the reference. However, it is recommended that the order of the names of each co-author be reversed because it is consistent with the general format of references to do so.

Ruby, A., Cashman, M. and Byrnes, M. 1992.
Targets, competencies and Australia's teachers.
Unicorn, 18 (1), 23–30.

Reversing the order of names and initials of all co-authors also assists the listing of references in alphabetical order. Where several references by the same author are listed, entries are ordered chronologically from oldest to most recent. Often entries need to be ordered alphabetically within a chronological sequence, but in such cases any works by a single author precede those works in which she or he is senior co-author:

Guthrie, J.T. 1981. Reading in New Zealand:
Achievement and volume. *Reading Research
Quarterly*, 17 (1), 6–27.

Guthrie, J.T. and Greaney, V. 1991. Literacy acts.
In R, Barr, M.L. Kamil, P. Mosenthal, and
P.D. Pearson (eds) *Handbook of Reading
Research* (Vol. 2, pp. 68–96), Longman,
New York.

Guthrie, J.T., Schafer, W.D., and Hutchinson,
S.R. 1991. Relations of document literacy and
prose literacy to occupational and societal
characteristics of young black and white
adults. *Reading Research Quarterly*, 26 (1),
30–48.

Guthrie, J.T. and Seifert, M. 1983. Profiles of
reading activity in a community. *Journal of
Reading*, 26 (4), 498–508.

A procedure that is not recommended is the practice of starting an entry with a solid line followed by a stop to indicate a second or subsequent work by the same author as the preceding work. Such a practice requires readers to refer upwards until they find the first entry giving the author's name in full. Little or no extra effort or cost is incurred in repeating the author's name for each reference by the same author. Such repetition adds clarity to a list of references.

If there is more than one entry for the same author in any one year, a lower case letter (a, b, c) immediately after the date differentiates between references. The order is given by the sequence in which the references are referred to in the text:

Shannon, P. 1990a. Joining the debate: Researchers and reading education curriculum. In J. Zutell and S. McCormick (eds), *Literacy Theory and Research*, National Reading Conference, Chicago.

Shannon, P. 1990b. *The Struggle to Continue: Progressive Reading Instruction in the 20th Century United States*, Heinemann, Portsmouth, NH.

Shannon, P. 1990c. The struggle for control of literacy lessons. *Language Arts*, 66, 625–634.

Some Special Cases

The next section presents a number of special cases. The examples serve as a guide to referencing format for translated works, works that are anonymous or where the author writes under a pseudonym, publications where an association or institution is author or where there is no author, proceedings of conferences, unpublished materials, theses and newspaper articles.

Translation of Another Author's Work

The translator's name is placed in brackets following the title of the work:

Davalo, E. and Naïm, P. 1991. *Neural Networks* (Translated by A. Rawsthorne). Macmillan, Basingstoke.

Anonymous Publication

Works of anonymous authors are alphabetised under their titles. If the author of an anonymous work is known, the name is placed in square brackets and entered in the reference under that name:

Politics in Fiji. 1992. *Current Affairs Bulletin*. 69 (6), 30–31.

[Dorward, D.] 1992. Crisis in Somalia: A failure for the United Nations and the new world order? *Current Affairs Bulletin*, 69 (6), 28–29.

Square brackets are commonly used since the writer is providing this information.

Pseudonymous Publication

Pseudonymous works are listed under the pseudonym with the author's name, where known, following in brackets:

> Vine, B. [Rendell, R.] 1987. *A Fatal Inversion.* Penguin, Harmondsworth.

Again, square brackets are used since the writer provides or adds this information.

Association or Institution as Author

Where an association or institution is author, the association/institution appears in the author position. The initials of the institution may be added where such information more readily identifies the institution:

> Australian Bureau of Statistics (ABS) 1984. *Classifications Manual for Government Finance Statistics, Australia.* Australian Government Publishing Service, Canberra.

Sometimes a country is added where there may be confusion with other countries that might have similarly named departments:

> Australia, Bureau of Transport and Communication Economics (BTCE) 1988. *Review of Road Cost Recovery.* Australian Government Publishing Service, Canberra.

Where the association/institution is both author and publisher, it is best to repeat the information in author and publisher positions:

> American Psychological Association 1994. *Publication Manual of the American Psychological Association* (4th ed.). American Psychological Association, Washington, DC.

No Author

Where there is no stated author, the title is placed in the author position:

> *Style Manual for Authors, Editors and Printers* (4th ed.) 1988. Australian Government Publishing Service, Canberra.

In the text, the form of reference is: *Style Manual for Authors, Editors and Printers* 1988. If unambiguous, the reference may simply be: *Style Manual* 1988 since this information is sufficient to locate the full reference in the list of references.

Conference Papers and Proceedings of Conferences

Papers presented at conferences have author and date followed by title of conference paper, name of conference, conference venue and dates:

> Blandy, R. 1993. The state of the Australian academic labour market. Paper presented to Conference on Higher Education and Immigration Issues, National Institute of Labour Studies, Adelaide, June 28.

Where proceedings of conferences are published, referencing follows the practice of an article in an edited work, with the association and venue for the conference included in the reference:

> Boissonnat, J.-D. 1992. Some new directions in robot motion planning. In van Leeuwen (ed.) *Algorithms, Software, Architecture: Information Processing* 92 (Vol. 1), North-Holland, Amsterdam, Proceedings of the IFIP 12th World Computer Congress, Madrid, September 7–11.

The hyphen in front of the second initial indicates a hyphenated name (here *Jean-Daniel*).

Unpublished Materials

Titles of unpublished materials are not italicised or underlined and are in sentence case:

> McGaw, B. 1993. Improving education and training research. Unpublished manuscript, Australian Council for Educational Research, Melbourne.

> Morrison, D.S. 1992. Case commentary: the Brick and Pipe Appeal – updating ostensible authorities. Paper read at the Corporate Law Teachers Conference, Canberra, February.

Theses

Theses are not considered published materials. Therefore, titles are not italicised or underlined and are in sentence case:

> Birkeland, J. 1992. Planning for a sustainable society. Unpublished doctoral thesis, University of Tasmania.

Koulouris, G. 1990. Measurement of low levels of ^{226}Ra in environmental waters using liquid scintillation counting. Unpublished Masters thesis, Queensland University of Technology.

Newspaper Articles

Newspaper or magazine articles are treated similarly to periodicals except that it is normal to precede the page numbers with the abbreviation *p.* or *pp.* as appropriate:

Denholm, M. 1997, April 14. Report card on schools' job success. *The Advertiser*, p. 1.

If an article continues to a non-consecutive page, all page numbers are indicated:

Walker, J. 1993, June 8. States face showdown over Mabo legal powers. *The Australian*, pp. 1-2, 11.

Where an article is in a section of a newspaper, page numbers may be preceded by the name of the section rather than the abbreviation for pages:

O'Neill, H. 1997, April 12-13. Crackers, hackers and their million-dollar backers. *The Weekend Australian*, Syte 1, 6.

Newspaper editorials and letters to the editor are distinguished from articles by inserting [Editorial] or [Letter to the Editor] after the title of the editorial or letter respectively:

Judicial debate is correct [Editorial]. 1997, April 15. *The Australian*, p. 14.

O'Leary, B. 1997, April 15. Gripe with grammar's latest fad [Letter to the Editor]. *The Australian*, p. 14.

Non-print Sources

Increasingly, writers need to refer to non-print as well as to printed sources. The final section of this chapter provides guidelines for referencing two main categories of non-print sources: (a) electronic media sources, such as computer programs, CD-ROMs, film and videotape, and (b) online information sources from the Internet and the World Wide Web.

Electronic Media Sources

Reference entries for a computer program, machine-readable data file, CD-ROM, film or videotape are identified by inserting in square brackets after the title a phrase specifying the non-print medium:

Anderson, J. 1996 *Text Detective* [Computer program]. Dataworks, Melbourne.

Hyde, M. 1993. *Shipwrecks Database* [Machine-readable data file]. Angle Park Computing Centre, Adelaide.

Libby, B. 1994. *Australian Walkabout* [CD-ROM]. Enville Holdings, Sydney.

Torrens Valley Institute of TAFE. 1994. *Switch On Learning: Using Technology in Adult Literacy and Basic Education* [Videotape]. Media Unit, Torrens Valley Institute of TAFE, Adelaide.

Online Sources

Because the World Wide Web is relatively new, conventions for referencing online sources are not as well established as conventions for referencing other electronic sources or printed works. However, the basic principles and the purposes are the same: to acknowledge one's indebtedness to others and to provide readers with sufficient information to locate the original source.

Considered first are ways to reference works that are published in print form but which are also available online. For such cases, the reference to the printed source is given in the usual way (author, date and publishing details). The type of medium is then indicated in square brackets, for example [Online], to indicate an Internet source. This is followed by the availability of the source in the form of its Web address or URL (see Chapter 6 for a discussion of Web addresses and Uniform Resource Locators or URLs). Finally, it is suggested that the date when the material was accessed be included also, again in square brackets.

Anderson, J. 1997. Australian College of Education review: 1996 in retrospect. *Unicorn*. Vol. 23, No. 1, 3–13. [Online] Available: http://wwwed.sturt. flinders.edu.au/Readings/Unicorn.html [1997, August 4]

Petre, D. and Harrington, D. 1996. *The Clever Country? Australia's Digital Future.* Lansdowne and Macmillan, Sydney. [1997, June 24, Book's Web site at http://www.ozfuture.com.nf]

In the last example, the Web address does not contain the full text of the work but rather a description of the main features and discussion of the work. Here, this supplementary information is placed in square brackets for the information of readers, to follow up if they wish.

Much information on the World Wide Web is available online only. Referencing of such materials is like referencing unpublished work, with the addition of [Online] to indicate the type of medium, followed by the Web address or URL where the work is available.

Spender, D. 1996. Creativity and the computer education industry. Paper presented to the International Federation for Information Processing Conference, Canberra, September 1996. [Online]. Available: http://www.acs.org.au/ifip96/dales.html [1997, July 1]

Worthington, T. 1996. Australia's 'Net Futures. Presentation for the National Press Club, 11 December 1996. [Online] Available: http://www.acs.org.au/president/1996/epubs/npctw.htm [1997, June 30]

Care needs to be taken when recording URLs. First, do not include any spaces in a URL. Second, be aware that URLs are case sensitive. Therefore, record upper case or lower case for components exactly.

C hapter **14**

APPENDIXES

The final part of an assignment or thesis, following the list of references, consists of materials to be placed in an appendix. This chapter describes the kind of materials commonly placed in appendixes and the formatting of appendixes.

Use of Appendix

The point is made in preceding chapters that a written paper (using this term for both assignments and theses) should aim at a high level of readability. This implies that only pertinent arguments should be included. There are times, however, when the inclusion of some relevant evidence or explanation in the body of the text would only serve to clutter it, rendering the argument more difficult to follow. By relegating such supporting evidence to an appendix, the text of a paper remains uncluttered; yet the argument is not weakened because the interested reader can be directed to consult particular pages of an appendix for further detail.

Each appendix should be referred to in the body of the paper. This is most directly done by reference in the text itself, or it may be noted in a footnote. Such reference should occur at the earliest point in the paper where the material appended is pertinent to the discussion. For example:

```
A copy of the test instructions is included in
Appendix A.
```

Subsequent reference also may be desirable. Ultimately, it is a matter of judgment whether to include material in an appendix or not. As a general principle, however, material should be appended if complete omission would tend to weaken the argument yet its inclusion in the body of the paper is not absolutely necessary to the text.

Pertinent material such as extensive quotations from evidence gathered, excerpts from diaries or transcripts from case studies, may appropriately be included in an appendix. If a data-gathering instrument such as a questionnaire or test of some kind has been used, a copy should be appended, together with any covering and follow-up letters. Statistical or raw data from which summary tables presented in the text are drawn should be included in an appendix. Where a detailed explanation is relevant to one section of a paper, but is not crucial to the whole, such explanation is often better placed in an appendix if it would tend to halt the flow of the text or be too expansive for a footnote. Also, usually it is desirable to append technical notes on experimental methods such as sampling procedures, illustrative materials or copies of computer programs used in data analysis.

Format of Appendix

A single appendix should be headed APPENDIX without punctuation, and positioned on a page in a similar way to major or chapter headings. An appendix desirably should have a title that usually is positioned three single spaces below the heading, also without punctuation:

APPENDIX

GLOSSARY OF TERMS

Where materials for inclusion in an appendix are numerous, it may be desirable to place each category of material into a separate appendix. Each appendix then should be separately identified and titled:

APPENDIX A

INSTRUCTIONS FOR ADMINISTRATION OF TESTS

Subsequent appendixes are then numbered B, C, and so on, each starting on a new page. It is optional whether the title for each appendix appears on a page by itself or whether the content follows immediately underneath. It is important, however, to be consistent.

Each page in the appendix is numbered consecutively with the rest of the paper, and margins should be maintained (see Chapter 9). Positioning of page numbers should be consistent with the rest of the paper. The nature of the material determines the spacing to be used in each appendix.

Appendixes are listed in the table of contents with commencing page numbers shown.

In theses, appendixes are placed immediately after the references or between the final chapter and the references. For assignments, appendixes normally follow the list of references. There is no fixed rule about placement, and it is largely left to the discretion of the research student as to which of these alternatives to follow.

Part III

REVISING THE ASSIGNMENT OR THESIS

EDITING AND EVALUATING THE FINAL PRODUCT

This chapter describes procedures for editing, evaluating and proofreading assignments and theses. A series of check lists is presented that are useful not only for the final stage of writing before submission but also for the initial stages when determining a consistent format.

Editing the Final Draft

Before the final draft of an assignment or thesis is printed, it should be carefully edited. It is the writer's responsibility to ensure that the text is free from spelling and grammatical errors. The spelling of unusual words should be checked in an authoritative dictionary. For questions of punctuation, capitalisation, hyphenation and abbreviations reference should be made to a recognised text of English language usage. See Chapter 1 and Appendix A for a list of resources for writers which includes Fowler's invaluable *Dictionary of Modern English Usage* and the standard reference to Australian spelling, the *Macquarie Dictionary*.

Word processors make light work of much of the careful checking necessary in the final draft of a paper. A spelling checker will detect most (but not all) spelling and typographical errors while the find and replace facility helps to achieve consistency as, for example, in replacing all *-iz-* spelling by *-is-* or ensuring that words like *program* are spelled consistently throughout a document. But a word processor is even more useful for adventurous editing of the kind where the order of phrases in sentences is altered perhaps to provide increased emphasis, or where the order of sentences within a paragraph, or paragraphs themselves, are interchanged to achieve greater clarity.

With a word processor, too, it is relatively straightforward to locate every author whose work has been cited and index these, or perhaps copy and paste to another file to form the basis of a list of references. Similarly, one can locate every table and figure in turn, copy the captions, and so ensure that the List of Tables and of Figures in the contents pages correspond with what appears in the text. Some word processors contain a feature for compiling a table of contents showing headings and levels of headings in a document, all with corresponding page numbers.

It is useful in revising and editing the final draft to carry out a number of systematic checks on such points as the use of headings and subheadings, quotations, footnotes, tables and figures, references and appendixes. The following check lists may prove useful in making these checks.

Check List for General Format

1. Is the paper or thesis divided clearly into preliminaries, text and reference material?
2. Are the *preliminaries*
   - in the correct sequence
   - in the correct format
   - numbered in small roman numerals?
3. Does the *title page* indicate
   - title of the paper
   - name of the author
   - name of the course, department, and faculty (where necessary)
   - name of the institution to which the paper is being submitted
   - date of submission
   - degree for which thesis is submitted?
4. Does the *table of contents* contain
   - an abstract or summary as appropriate
   - acknowledgments
   - list of tables
   - list of figures
   - bibliography or references
   - appendixes?
5. Is the *main text*
   - carefully organised with subheadings matching the headings in the table of contents
   - properly sequenced with chapter headings matching those in the table of contents
   - structured with a carefully designed introduction and conclusion?

6. Is the *reference material*
   - subdivided (where necessary) in the bibliography
   - given a title (where necessary)?
7. Have the requirements of the institution been checked regarding
   - number of copies
   - binding
   - colour of cover
   - lettering on cover?

Check List for Headings and Subheadings

1. Are headings and subheadings formatted consistently throughout the assignment or thesis?
2. Are chapter *designations and numbers*
   - consistently spaced from the top of the page
   - consistently formatted as level 1 headings
   - numbered with arabic numerals?
3. Are *chapter titles*
   - consistently formatted as level 1 headings
   - double spaced below chapter designation and number
   - three single spaces above the next heading or first line of text?
4. Are *centred headings* (*if* used)
   - separated from the text above and below by three single spaces
   - in lower case except for the first letter of the first word and of all key words
   - at least two to a chapter?
5. Are all side *headings*
   - flush with left-hand margin
   - consistently formatted according to number of levels of headings
   - in caption form and without periods?

Check List for Quotations

1. Have quotations been assessed for
   - relevance
   - forceful expression
   - validating an argument
   - providing a basis for discussion or critical analysis?
2. Have extracts copied verbatim been checked for accuracy in
   - spelling
   - punctuation
   - capitalisation
   - word order?

3. Where an extract is modified, is this shown by
   - interpolation and the use of square brackets
   - ellipsis?
4. Are long quotations
   - single spaced and indented
   - appropriately introduced?
5. Is each quotation accurately referenced?

Check List for Footnotes

1. Does the footnote
   - validate or amplify a point
   - acknowledge indebtedness for an idea
   - give the interested reader enough information to follow a source to greater depth
   - provide a suitable cross-reference
   - acknowledge a direct or indirect quotation?
2. Is the footnote complete with
   - name of author
   - title of source
   - page references
   - date of publication?
3. Is the placement of footnotes consistent at the
   - foot of each page
   - end of each chapter
   - end of the paper?
4. Is repetitious and bulky footnoting avoided by conventions such as
   - ibid.
   - op. cit.
   - loc. cit.?
5. Are footnote numbers
   - in arabic numerals (except for mathematical texts or tables)
   - in superscripts
   - without punctuation?
6. Is the reference system adopted in footnotes consistent?
7. In citing the author, does the first name or initial precede the surname?
8. Is each footnote concluded with a period?
9. Are footnotes separated from the main body of the text?
10. Are footnotes single-spaced, but separated from other footnotes by a double space?

Check List for Tables

1. Is the table warranted?
2. Have the data been checked?
3. Is the table positioned close to but following its mention in the text?

4. Is the table appropriately included in the text or an appendix?
5. Are tables numbered consecutively?
6. Are sufficient details given to interpret the table?
7. Is the table number and caption above the table?
8. Does the table caption detail the table contents sufficiently?
9. Does the wording of the caption correspond to that given in the List of Tables?
10. Is a consistent format used for all tables?
11. Is the wording for the stub boxhead and field boxhead(s) contained in the table caption?
12. Are units of measurement stated?
13. Are abbreviations explained in the table?
14. Could the table be presented more simply?
15. Are column entries correctly aligned?
16. Is footnote usage consistent?
17. Is the top of any table printed on its side at the binding edge?
18. Have the conventions for continued tables been followed?
19. Is the table correctly positioned on the page?
20. Is the page number shown?

Check List for Figures

1. Does the figure contribute to the presentation?
2. Has the accuracy of the figure been checked?
3. Is the figure positioned close to but following its mention in the text?
4. Are figures numbered consecutively?
5. Is the figure self-explanatory?
6. Is the figure number and caption *below* the figure?
7. Does the figure caption detail the contents of the figure sufficiently?
8. Does the wording of the caption correspond to that given in the List of Figures?
9. Are vertical and horizontal axes of graphs labelled?
10. Is the zero position on the vertical axis of graphs shown?
11. Are the units of measurement indicated and clearly shown on axes?
12. Are the separate observations comprising any graph marked?
13. Are all components of the figure clearly labelled?
14. Are all abbreviations explained in the figure?
15. Does the arrangement of the figure proceed from left to right?
16. Are the numerical data from which the figure was drawn given (not necessarily with figure)?
17. Can the figure be easily read?
18. Is the figure correctly positioned on the page?
19. Is the page number shown?

Check List for Referencing

1. Is the *heading*
   - formatted and positioned appropriately
   - without punctuation?
2. Has each page of the references been numbered?
3. Has every work cited been included in the list of references?
4. Have the rules for alphabetical and chronological ordering of references been consistently followed?
5. Have institutional requirements for referencing format been met?
6. Does each *book* reference include
   - author(s)
   - date of publication
   - title of book (from title page)
   - publisher
   - place of publication?
7. Does each *periodical* reference include
   - author(s)
   - date of publication
   - title of article
   - name of journal
   - volume number (and, if available, issue number)
   - inclusive page numbers?
8. Do references to non-print sources include the type of medium enclosed in square brackets following the title?
9. Do references to online sources include URLs, carefully checked and without spaces?
10. Have the rules for spacing, sequencing, capitalisation and use of italics been consistently followed?
11. Is the list of references correctly placed?

Check List for Appendixes

1. Is the body of the thesis unnecessarily cluttered?
2. What material in the text of the thesis, if any, might better be placed in an appendix?
3. Is the argument weakened by appending material which should be included in the text?
4. Is the appendix warranted?
5. Is the appendix referred to in the text?
6. Is reference to the appendix made at the earliest point in the thesis where the material appended is relevant to the discussion?
7. Is subsequent reference to the appendix desirable?
8. Have any raw data collected in the study been appended?

9. Have copies of data-gathering instruments, and of covering and follow-up letters, been appended?
10. Are technical notes and explanations of experimental procedures appended?
11. Has the accuracy of the appendix been checked?
12. Are sufficient details given to interpret the appendix?
13. Can the appendix be easily read?
14. Does each appendix start a new page?
15. Are appendixes lettered consecutively?
16. Does the title of the appendix correspond to that listed in the Table of Contents?
17. Is the title of the appendix correctly positioned without punctuation?
18. Is the appendix correctly placed?
19. Has each page in the appendix been given a number?

Evaluating the Final Draft

Throughout the revising and rewriting of the several drafts of an assignment or thesis it is necessary to examine the work critically, to be detached, and to see it as others might see it. Experienced writers commonly report how valuable it is to leave a period of time to intervene between the penultimate and the final draft. The passing of time helps to separate writers from their work. This serves to give that feeling of detachment that is so necessary to assess critically the expression and organisation of one's ideas.

Writers also need to evaluate their writing against the recognised canons of research. The following two check lists may prove useful in providing criteria for evaluating research reports. The first is more suited to the empirical/experimental study, and the second to the analytical/literary study. Not all the criteria will be applicable to every study but the check lists may be adapted to meet particular needs.

Check List for Evaluating Empirical/Experimental Research Studies

Problem
1. Is the problem clearly stated?
2. Is the problem significant — will the results contribute to the solution of some practical or theoretical problem?
3. Are the hypotheses clearly stated?
4. Are the hypotheses logically deduced from some theory or problem?
5. Is the relationship to previous research made clear?

Design

6. Are the assumptions of the study clearly stated?
7. Are the limitations of the study stated?
8. Are important terms in the study defined?
9. Is the research design fully described?
10. Is the research design appropriate?
11. Are the population and sample described?
12. Is the method of sampling appropriate?
13. Are the controls described and appropriate?
14. Is the research design free of weaknesses?

Procedure

15. Are the data-gathering methods described?
16. Are the data-gathering methods appropriate?
17. Are the data-gathering methods properly used?
18. Are the validity and reliability of the evidence established?

Analysis

19. Are the methods of analysis appropriate and are they properly applied?
20. Are the results of the analysis clearly presented?

Conclusions

21. Are the conclusions clearly stated?
22. Are the conclusions substantiated by the evidence presented?
23. Are the generalisations confined to the population from which the sample was drawn?
24. Is the report logically organised and clearly written?
25. Is the tone of the report impartial and scientific?

Check List for Evaluating Analytical/Literary Research Studies

Objectives

1. Are the purposes of the study stated clearly?
2. Does the study make a contribution to existing knowledge?
3. Is the background to the study clearly described?
4. Have previous studies in the field relevant to the thesis been evaluated?

Procedures

5. Are the underlying assumptions clearly stated?
6. Are the limitations to the study stated?
7. Are important terms in the study defined?
8. Are the methods for locating source materials described?

9. Have the appropriate source materials been selected?
10. Has the quality of the source materials been assessed?
11. Are the source materials clearly documented?
12. Has the reliability of the evidence been established?

Analysis
13. Are all pertinent facts included in the analysis?
14. Have all source materials been critically evaluated?
15. Is the logic of the argument sound?
16. Is the interpretation of findings clear?

Conclusions
17. Are the findings clearly stated?
18. Are the conclusions substantiated by the evidence presented?
19. Is the report logically organised?
20. Is the report clearly written?

Proofreading the Final Printed Copy

After an assignment or thesis has been printed for what, hopefully, is the last time, it is still necessary to carry out a few final checks. First, proofread each page carefully. Spelling checkers do not detect all errors. Errors in the spellings of names will obviously not be indicated. A special check should be made next of the correct syllabic division of words at the end of lines if words have been divided between lines. Fortunately, with a word processor it is quick to reprint a page, without the need for extensive retyping.

Special symbols not available on a particular word processor or printer may need to be inserted in a document. Such insertions should be in india ink. It is important to check one last time that the page numbers in the Table of Contents, List of Tables and List of Figures correspond exactly with headings, tables and figures in the text. Finally, before binding or attaching the pages together in some way, a check should be made that pages are in correct sequence.

Appendix **A**

ADDITIONAL RESOURCES
FOR WRITERS

Chapter 1 contains a short list of essential resources for writers. Publishing details are given below, together with further works focusing on different aspects of scholarly writing. Since language and its conventions are in a process of continuous change, dates and edition numbers are not shown. It is important to seek out the latest editions of such reference texts.

English Expression

Bate, D. and Sharpe, P. *Essay Method and English Expression*. Harcourt Brace Jovanovich, Sydney.

Fowler, H. W. *A Dictionary of Modern English Usage*. Oxford University Press, Oxford.

Gatherer, W. A. *The Student's Handbook of Modern English*. Holmes McDougall, Edinburgh.

Gordon, I. *Punctuation*. Longman, London.

Hudson, N. *Modern Australian Usage*. Oxford University Press, Melbourne.

Murray-Smith, S. *Right Words: A Guide to English Usage in Australia*. Viking, Melbourne.

Osland, D., Boyd, D., McKenna, W. and Salusinszky, I. *Writing in Australia*. Harcourt Brace Jovanovich, Sydney.

Partridge, E. *Usage and Abusage: A Guide to Good English*. Penguin, Harmondsworth.

Peters, P. *The Cambridge Australian English Style Guide*. Cambridge University Press, Cambridge.

Sorrels, B. D. *The Nonsexist Communicator: Solving the Problems of Gender and Awkwardness in Modern English*. Prentice Hall, Englewood Cliffs, NJ.

Wood, F. T. *Current English Usage* (rev.ed.). Macmillan, London.

Dictionaries and Thesauri

Collins COBUILD English Language Dictionary. Collins, London.

Roget, S. M. *Roget's Thesaurus of Words and Phrases*. Macmillan, Melbourne.

The Macquarie Dictionary. The Macquarie Library, Sydney.

The Macquarie Thesaurus: The Book of Words. The Macquarie Library, Sydney.

Essay, Report and Thesis Writing

Bate, D. and Sharpe, P. *Student Writer's Handbook*. Harcourt Brace Jovanovich, Sydney.

Berry, R. *How to Write a Research Paper*. Pergamon Press, London.

Campbell, W. G., Ballou, S. V. and Slade, S. *Form and Style: Theses, Reports, Term Papers*. Houghton Mifflin, Boston.

Clanchy, J. and Ballard, B. *Essay Writing for Students*. Longman Cheshire, Melbourne.

Cooper, B. C. *Writing Technical Reports*. Penguin, Harmondsworth.

Lewins, F. *Writing a Thesis: A Guide to its Nature and Organisation*. Australian National University, Canberra.

Peters, P. *Strategies for Student Writers*. John Wiley and Sons, Brisbane.

Ruhl, J. *The Writer's Toolbox*. Prentice Hall, Englewood Cliffs, NJ.

Turabian, Kate L. and Honigsblum, B. *A Manual for Writers of Term Papers, Theses and Dissertations*. University of Chicago Press, Chicago.

Style Manuals

Li, X. and Crane, N. B. *Electronic Styles: A Handbook for Citing Electronic Information*. Information Today, Medford, NJ.

Modern Humanities Research Association. *MHRA Style Book: Notes for Authors, Editors, and Writers of Theses*. Modern Humanities Research Association, London.

Style Manual for Authors, Editors and Printers. Australian Government Publishing Service, Canberra.

The Chicago Manual of Style. University of Chicago Press, Chicago.

van Leunen, M. *A Handbook for Scholars*. Oxford University Press, Oxford.

Manuals for Particular Disciplines

Achtert, S. and Gibaldi, J. *The MLA Style Manual*. Modern Language Association, New York.

American Chemical Society. *Handbook for Authors*. American Chemical Society Publications, Washington.

American Geographical Union. *AGU Style: A Guide for Contributors*. American Geographical Union, Washington.

American Institute of Biological Sciences. *Style Manual for Biological Journals*. Conference of Biological Editors, American Institute of Biological Sciences, Washington.

American Institute of Physics. *Style Manual for Guidance in the Preparation of Papers*. American Institute of Physics, New York.

American Psychological Association. *Publication Manual of the American Psychological Association*. American Psychological Association, Washington.

Freeman, T. W. *The Writing of Geography*. Manchester University Press, Manchester.

Gelfand, H. and Walker, C. J. *Mastering APA Style: Instructor's Resource Guide*. American Psychological Association, Washington.

Grinsell, L., Rahtz, P. and Williams, D. P. *The Preparation of Archaeological Reports*. St. Martin's Press, New York.

Huth, E. J. *Medical Style and Format: An International Manual for Authors, Editors and Publishers*. ISI Press, Philadelphia.

May, C. A. *Effective Writing: A Handbook for Accountants*. Prentice Hall, Englewood Cliffs, NJ.

Morgan, P. *An Insider's Guide for Medical Authors and Editors*. ISI Press, Philadelphia.

O'Shea, R. P. *Writing for Psychology: An Introductory Guide for Students*. Harcourt Brace Jovanovich, Sydney.

Smyth, T. R. *Writing in Psychology: A Student Guide*. John Wiley, Brisbane.

Swanson, E. *Mathematics into Type*. American Mathematical Society, Providence, RI.

Internet Resources

Because of the rapid rate of change in information technology, dates are included for the following small selection of the burgeoning available resources for the Internet and the World Wide Web.

Gilster, P. 1997. *Digital Literacy*. John Wiley, New York.

Petre, D. and Harrington, D. 1996. *The Clever Country? Australia's Digital Future*. Landsdowne and Macmillan, Sydney.

Reddick, R. and King, E. 1996. *The Online Student: Making the Grade on the Internet*. Harcourt Brace, New York.

Seltzer, R., Ray, E. J. and Ray, D. S. 1997. *The AltaVista Search Revolution*. Osborne McGraw-Hill, Berkeley.

Snyder, I. 1996. *Hypertext: The Electronic Labyrinth*, Melbourne University Press, Melbourne.

The World Wide Web Walkabout. [Online] Available: http://www.lib.mq.edu.au/wwww/welcome.html

Appendix B

ABBREVIATIONS COMMONLY USED IN SCHOLARLY WRITING

Many abbreviations, mostly of Latin origin, and certain special symbols are encountered in scholarly writing. Table B.1 presents the meanings of the most common of these together with examples where appropriate.

Table B.1 Meanings and examples of abbreviations, terms and symbols encountered in scholarly writing

Abbreviation	Meaning and Example
anon.	anonymous (used when the author is not known)
Art.	Article e.g. Art. 4
aug.	augmented; enlarged
Bk.	Book e.g. Bk. 2
[ ]	square brackets (used around words inserted within quotes or where additional information is inserted by writers in references)
bull.	bulletin
c. or ca.	circa; about or approximately (used to refer to dates)

Continued

Abbreviation	Meaning and Example
cf.	confer; compare e.g. cf. Table 2 on page 20
Chap(s).	chapter(s) e.g. in Chap. 1
col(s).	column(s) e.g. see cols 1–3
ed(s).	editor(s) or edited e.g. Collins, C. 1993 (ed.); edition e.g. 3rd ed.
e.g.	exempli gratia; for example
enl.	enlarged
et al.	et alii; and others (used to refer to co-authors when there are four or more) e.g. Miller et al.
et alibi	and elsewhere
et seq.	et sequens; and the following
f., ff.	the page, pages following e.g. p. 4f.– page 4 and the following page; p. 4ff. – page 4 and the following pages till the subject is finished
Fig(s).	Figure(s) e.g. Fig. 3
ibid.	ibidem; in the same place or work (used when two or more successive footnotes refer to the same work; if reference is to different pages, page numbers are indicated)
idem	the same (used when a footnote refers to the same work and the same page as the previous footnote)
i.e.	id est; that is
infra	below (used to refer to text following)
l., ll.	line, lines e.g. l. 10; ll. 10–12
loc. cit.	loco citato; in the place cited (used when reference is made to the same place, that is the same page, as a preceding but not immediately preceding reference; used with last name of author only)

Continued

Abbreviation	Meaning and Example
MS., MSS.	manuscript, manuscripts
n., nn.	note or footnote, notes or footnotes e.g. n. 2; nn. 3 and 4
N.B.	nota bene; note well
n.d.	no date of publication given
No(s).	number(s) e.g. No. 4; Nos 3–5
non seq.	non sequitur; it does not follow
n.p.	no place of publication given
op. cit.	opere citato; in the work cited (used when reference is made to the same work as a preceding but not immediately preceding reference; abbreviation follows author's name but precedes page reference)
p., pp.	page, pages e.g. p. 40; pp. 71–74
par(s).	paragraph(s) e.g. par. 4; pars 4–6
passim	here and there (generally used to refer to opinions or attitudes over a number of different pages)
P.S.	postscriptum; postscript
Pt(s).	part(s) e.g. Pt. III, Pts I and II
q.v.	quod vide; which see
rev.	revised or revision
rev. ed.	revised edition
sec(s).	section(s) e.g. sec. 4; secs 6–8
[sic]	thus (used to call attention to the fact that an error in spelling, grammar, or fact is in the original; enclosed by square brackets and placed immediately after the word or phrase in question)
supra	above (used to refer to text already cited)
trans.	translator, translated, translation
vid or vide	see
vide infra	see below

Continued

Abbreviation	Meaning and Example
vide supra	see above
v., vv.	verse, verses
viz.	videlicet; namely
vol(s).	volume (used for number of volumes e.g. 3 vols)
Vol(s).	volume(s) (used for Volume number e.g. Vol. I, Vols II-IV)
vs.	versus; against

INDEX